# SKILLS
## FOR SUCCESS
## with Integrated Projects
*Getting Started*

# SKILLS
## FOR SUCCESS
## with Integrated Projects
*Getting Started*

**CATHERINE HAIN**

**PEARSON**

Upper Saddle River, New Jersey, 07458

**Library of Congress Cataloging-in-Publication Data**

Hain, Catherine.
Skills for success : getting started with integrated projects / by Catherine Hain.
    p. cm.
  Includes bibliographical references and index.
  ISBN-13: 978-0-13-504038-6
  ISBN-10: 0-13-504038-8
  1. Integrated software.    2. Microsoft software.    I. Title.
QA76.76.I57H34 2008
005.3—dc22                                    2008026225

**VP/Publisher:** *Natalie E. Anderson*
**Editor in Chief:** *Michael Payne*
**Associate VP/ Executive Acquisitions Editor,**
    **Print:** *Stephanie Wall*
**Director, Product Development:** *Pamela Hersperger*
**Product Development Manager:** *Eileen Bien Calabro*
**Editorial Project Manager:** *Meghan Bisi*
**Editorial Assistant:** *Terenia McHenry*
**AVP/Executive Editor, Media:** *Richard Keaveny*
**AVP/Executive Producer:** *Lisa Strite*
**Editorial Media Project Manager:** *Alana Coles*
**Production Media Project Manager:** *Lorena Cerisano*
**Marketing Manager:** *Tori Olson Alves*
**Marketing Assistant:** *Angela Frey*
**Senior Managing Editor:** *Cynthia Zonneveld*

**Associate Managing Editor:** *Camille Trentacoste*
**Production Project Manager:** *Ruth Ferrera-Kargov*
**Manager of Rights & Permissions:** *Charles Morris*
**Senior Operations Specialist:** *Nick Sklitsis*
**Operations Specialist:** *Natacha St. Hill Moore*
**Senior Art Director:** *Jonathan Boylan*
**Art Director:** *Anthony Gemmellaro*
**Composition:** *GGS Book Services PMG*
**Full-Service Project Management:**
    *GGS Book Services PMG*
  **Cover Printer:** *Phoenix Color*
**Printer/Binder:** *Quad/graphics Taunton*
**Typeface:** *10/12 Minion Regular*

Pearson Education Ltd., London
Pearson Education Singapore, Pte. Ltd
Pearson Education, Canada, Inc.
Pearson Education—Japan

Pearson Education Australia PTY, Limited
Pearson Education North Asia Ltd., Hong Kong.
Pearson Educación de Mexico, S.A. de C.V.
Pearson Education, Malaysia, Pte. Ltd.

**Prentice Hall**
is an imprint of

www.prenhall.com/skills

10 9 8 7 6 5
ISBN-10: 0-13-504038-8
ISBN-13: 978-0-13-504038-6

# Table of Contents

# Contributors

We'd like to thank the following people for their work on Skills for Success:

## Instructor Resource Authors

Linda Arnold, Harrisburg Area Community College
LaDonna Bachand, Santa Rosa Community College
Sharon Behrens, Northeast Wisconsin Technical College
Sue Birtwell, Kwantlen University College
Nancy Boito, Harrisburg Area Community College
Lynn Bowen, Valdosta Technical College
Diane Coyle, Montgomery County Community College
Loorna De Duluc, Miami Dade College
Dennis Faiz, Harrisburg Area Community College
Linda Foster-Turpen, Central New Mexico Community College
Debra Geoghan, Bucks County Community College

Jessica Gilmore, Highline Community College
Kermelle Hensley, Columbus Technical College
Stephanie Jones, South Plains College
Kelli Kleindorfer, American Institute of Business
Catherine Laberta, Erie Community College
Andrea Leinbach, Harrisburg Area Community College
Donna Madsen, Kirkwood Community College
Trina Maurer, Georgia Virtual Technical College
Phil Vavalides, Guilford Tech Community College
Dawn Wood, Technically Speaking Consultants

## Technical Editors

Colette Eisele         Jan Snyder
Joyce Nielsen          June West
Janet Pickard          Mara Zebest

## Reviewers

Laurel Aagard, Sierra College
John Alcorcha, MTI College
Barry Andrews, Miami Dade College
Natalie Andrews, Sinclair Community College
Wilma Andrews, Virginia Commonwealth University School of Business
Bridget Archer, Oakton Community College
Greg Ballinger, Miami Dade College
Terry Bass, University of Massachusetts, Lowell
Rocky Belcher, Sinclair Community College
Nannette Bibby, Miami Dade College
Alisa Brown, Pulaski Technical College
Eric Cameron, Passaic Community College
Trey Cherry, Edgecombe Community College
Kim Childs, Bethany University
Pauline Chohonis, Miami Dade College
Lennie Cooper, Miami Dade College
Gail Cope, Sinclair Community College
Chris Corbin, Miami Dade College

Tommi Crawford, Miami Dade College
Martin Cronlund, Anne Arundel Community College
Jennifer Day, Sinclair Community College
Ralph DeArazoza, Miami Dade College
Loorna DeDuluc, Miami Dade College
Caroline Delcourt, Black Hawk College
Michael Discello, Pittsburgh Technical Institute
Kevin Duggan, Midlands Technical Community College
Barbara Edington, St. Francis College
Donna Ehrhart, Genesee Community College
Tushnelda Fernandez, Miami Dade College
Arlene Flerchinger, Chattanooga State Tech Community College
Hedy Fossenkemper, Paradise Valley Community College
Kent Foster, Winthrop University
Arlene Franklin, Bucks County Community College
George Gabb, Miami Dade College
Deb Geoghan, Bucks County Community College
Jessica Gilmore, Highline Community College

Victor Giol, Miami Dade College

Linda Glassburn, Cuyahoga Community College, West

Deb Gross, Ohio State University

Rachelle Hall, Glendale Community College

Marie Hartlein, Montgomery County Community College

Diane Hartman, Utah Valley State College

Patrick Healy, Northern Virginia Community College-Woodbridge

Lindsay Henning, Yavapai College

Kermelle Hensley, Columbus Technical College

Mary Carole Hollingsworth, GA Perimeter

Stacey Gee Hollins, St. Louis Community College—Meramec

Joan Ivey, Lanier Technical College

Kay Johnston, Columbia Basin College

Sally Kaskocsak, Sinclair Community College

Hazel Kates, Miami Dade College

Charles Kellermann, Northern Virginia Community College—Woodbridge

John Kidd, Tarrant County Community College

Chris Kinnard, Miami Dade College

Kelli Kleindorfer, American Institute of Business

Kurt Kominek, Northeast State Technical Community College

Dianne Kotokoff, Lanier Technical College

Jean Lacoste, Virginia Tech

Gene Laughrey, Northern Oklahoma College

David LeBron, Miami Dade College

Kaiyang Liang, Miami Dade College

Linda Lindaman, Black Hawk College

Felix Lopez, Miami Dade College

Nicki Maines, Mesa Community College

Cindy Manning, Big Sandy Community and Technical College

Patri Mays, Paradise Valley Community College

Sandy McCormack, Monroe Community College

Lee McKinley, GA Perimeter

Eric Meyer, Miami Dade College

Jackie Meyers, Sinclair Community College

Kathryn Miller, Big Sandy Community and Technical College, Pikeville Campus

Kathy Morris, University of Alabama, Tuscaloosa

Linda Moulton, Montgomery County Community College

Ryan Murphy, Sinclair Community College

Stephanie Murre Wolf, Moraine Park Technical College

Jackie Myers, Sinclair Community College

Dell Najera, El Paso Community College, Valle Verde Campus

Scott Nason, Rowan Cabarrus Community College

Paula Neal, Sinclair Community College

Eloise Newsome, Northern Virginia Community College—Woodbridge

Ellen Orr, Seminole Community College

Carol Ottaway, Chemeketa Community College

Denise Passero, Fulton-Montgomery Community College

Janet Pickard, Chattanooga State Tech Community College

Floyd Pittman, Miami Dade College

Melissa Prinzing, Sierra College

Pat Rahmlow, Montgomery County Community College

Kamaljeet Sanghera, George Mason University

Teresa Sept, College of Southern Idaho

Gary Sibbits, St. Louis Community College—Meramec

Janet Siert, Ellsworth Community College

Robert Sindt, Johnson County Community College

Robert Smolenski, Delaware County Community College

Patricia Snyder, Midlands Technical Community College

Diane Stark, Phoenix College

Linda Stoudemayer, Lamar Institute of Technology

Linda Switzer, Highline Community College

Margaret Taylor, College of Southern Nevada

Martha Taylor, Sinclair Community College

Roseann Thomas, Fayetteville Tech Community College

Ingrid Thompson-Sellers, GA Perimeter

Daniel Thomson, Keiser University

Barb Tollinger, Sinclair Community College

Cathy Urbanski, Chandler Gilbert Community College

Philip Vavalides, Guilford Technical Community College

Pete Vetere, Montgomery County Community College—West Campus

Asteria Villegas, Monroe College

Michael Walton, Miami Dade College

Teri Weston, Harford Community College

Julie Wheeler, Sinclair Community College

Debbie Wood, Western Piedmont Community College

Thomas Yip, Passaic Community College

Matt Zullo, Wake Technical Community College

# About the Author

**Catherine Hain** is an instructor at Central New Mexico Community College in Albuquerque, New Mexico. She teaches computer applications classes in the Business and Information Technology School, both in the classroom and through the distance learning office. Catherine holds a bachelor's degree in Management and Marketing and a master's in Business Administration.

*For the love and laughter you bring to my life, this book is dedicated to my husband Tom and to my sisters and brothers: Carol, Jerry, Raymond, Joe, Alice, David, Janet, Jim, Margaret, Richard, and JoAnn.*

—CATHERINE HAIN

A textbook that recognizes how students learn today–

# Skills for Success
### with Integrated Projects Getting Started

- **10 x 8 Format –** Easy for students to read and type at the same time by simply propping the book up on the desk in front of their monitor

- **Clearly Outlined Skills –** Each skill is presented in a single two-page spread so that students can easily follow along

- **Numbered Steps and Bulleted Text –** Students don't read long paragraphs or text, but they will read information presented concisely

- **Easy-to-Find Student Data Files –** Visual key shows students how to locate and interact with their data files

**Start Here –** Students know exactly where to start and what their starting file will look like

**Outcome –** Shows students up front what their completed project will look like

**Skills List –** A visual snapshot of what skills they will complete in the chapter

**Sequential Pagination –** Saves you and your students time in locating topics and assignments

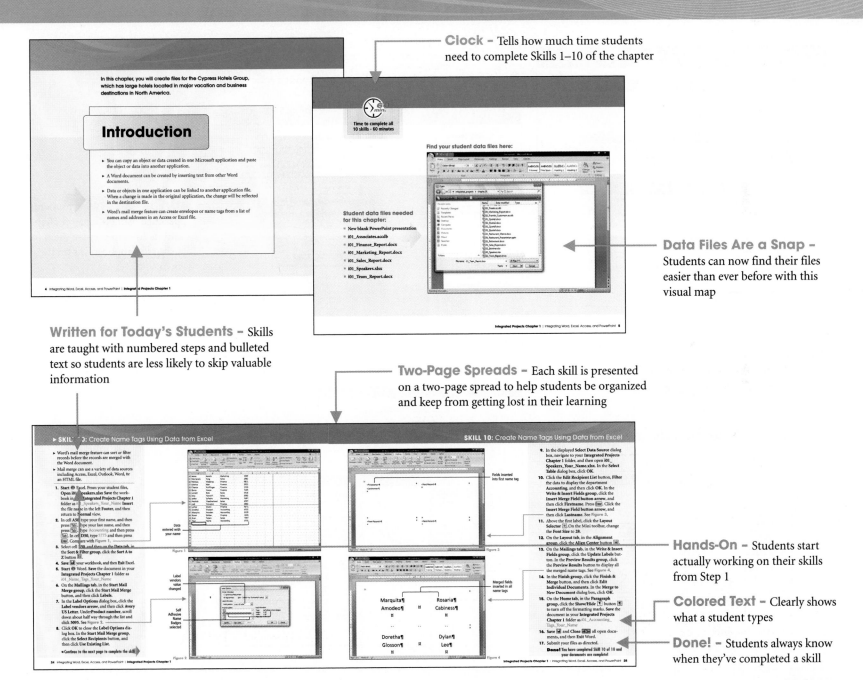

**Clock** – Tells how much time students need to complete Skills 1–10 of the chapter

**Data Files Are a Snap** – Students can now find their files easier than ever before with this visual map

**Written for Today's Students** – Skills are taught with numbered steps and bulleted text so students are less likely to skip valuable information

**Two-Page Spreads** – Each skill is presented on a two-page spread to help students be organized and keep from getting lost in their learning

**Hands-On** – Students start actually working on their skills from Step 1

**Colored Text** – Clearly shows what a student types

**Done!** – Students always know when they've completed a skill

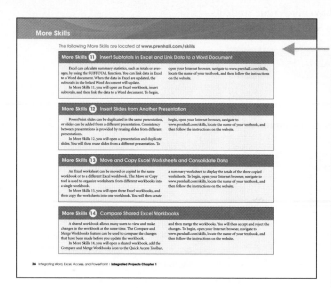

**More Skills** – Additional skills included online

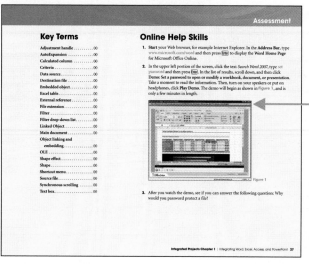

**Online Project** – Students practice using Microsoft Help online to help prepare them for using the applications on their own

**End-of-Chapter Material** – Several levels of assessment so you can assign the material that best fits your students' needs

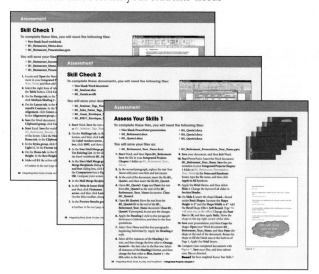

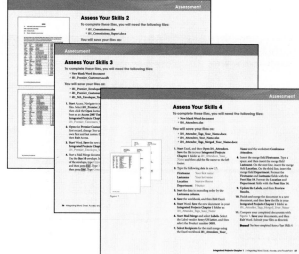

# Instructor Materials

**All Instructor materials available online**

**Instructor's Manual -** Teaching tips and additional resources for each chapter

**Assignment Sheets -** Lists all the assignments for the chapter, you just add in the course information, due dates, and points. Providing these to students ensures they will know what is due and when

**Assignment Tags -** Can be used either by students to check their work or by you as a quick check-off for the items that need to be corrected

**Scripted Lectures -** Classroom lectures prepared for you

**Annotated Solution Files -** Coupled with the assignment tags this creates a grading and scoring system that makes grading so much easier for you

**PowerPoint Lectures -** PowerPoint presentations for each chapter

**Prepared Exams -** Exams for each chapter

**Test Bank -** Includes a variety of test questions for each chapter

# SKILLS
## FOR SUCCESS

**with Integrated Projects**
*Getting Started*

# CHAPTER 1

# Integrating Word, Excel, Access, and PowerPoint

► Microsoft Office is an integrated program suite—the data and objects in one application can be used in another application.

► Data and objects can be copied and pasted, moved, linked, or embedded between the applications.

## Your starting screen will look similar to this:

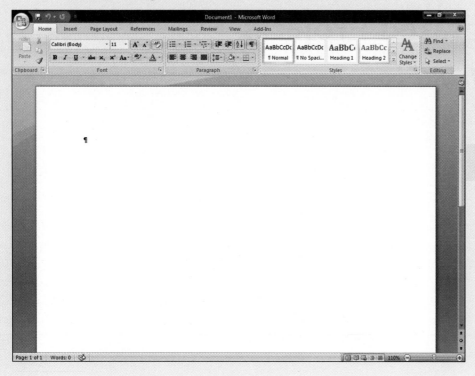

## SKILLS

**At the end of this chapter, you will be able to:**

**Skill 1** Move Text Between Word Documents
**Skill 2** Apply Heading Styles in Word
**Skill 3** Create a PowerPoint Presentation from a Word Document
**Skill 4** Insert and Modify a Shape in PowerPoint
**Skill 5** Import a Word Table into an Excel Workbook
**Skill 6** Insert a Shape from PowerPoint into Word and Excel
**Skill 7** Create and Work with an Excel Table
**Skill 8** Link Data Between Office Applications using OLE
**Skill 9** Create Envelopes Using Data from Access
**Skill 10** Create Name Tags Using Data from Excel

### MORE SKILLS

**More Skills 11** Insert Subtotals in Excel and Link Data to a Word Document
**More Skills 12** Insert Slides from Another Presentation
**More Skills 13** Move and Copy Excel Worksheets and Consolidate Data
**More Skills 14** Compare Shared Excel Workbooks

## Outcome

Using the skills listed to the left will enable you to create documents like this:

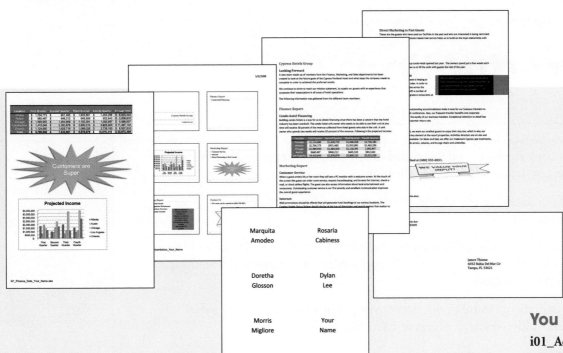

## You will save these files as:

i01_Accounting_Tags_Your_Name.docx

i01_Envelopes_Merged_Your_Name.docx

i01_Envelopes_Your_Name.docx

i01_Finance_Data_Your_Name.xlsx

i01_Name_Tags_Your_Name.docx

i01_Speakers_Your_Name.xlsx

i01_Team_Presentation_Your_Name.pptx

i01_Team_Report_Your_Name.docx

In this chapter, you will create files for the Cypress Hotels Group, which has large hotels located in major vacation and business destinations in North America.

# Introduction

- ▶ You can copy an object or data created in one Microsoft application and paste the object or data into another application.

- ▶ A Word document can be created by inserting text from other Word documents.

- ▶ Data or objects in one application can be linked to another application file. When a change is made in the original application, the change will be reflected in the destination file.

- ▶ Word's mail merge feature can create envelopes or name tags from a list of names and addresses in an Access or Excel file.

Time to complete all
10 skills - 60 minutes

## Find your student data files here:

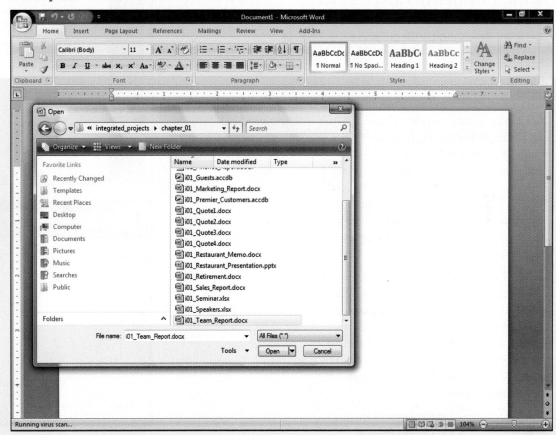

## Student data files needed for this chapter:

- New blank PowerPoint presentation
- i01_Associates.accdb
- i01_Finance_Report.docx
- i01_Marketing_Report.docx
- i01_Sales_Report.docx
- i01_Speakers.xlsx
- i01_Team_Report.docx

▶ Text from one Word document can be inserted into another document.

1. Click **Start** 🔘. Click **Control Panel**, and then click **Appearance and Personalization**. Under **Folder Options**, click **Show hidden files and folders**. Under **Advanced settings**, clear the **Hide extensions for known file types** check box. Click **OK**, and then click the **Close** button 🔳.

   This setting will display *file extensions*—a set of characters added to the end of file names that identifies each file type—in all folder windows and window title bars.

2. **Start** 🔘 Word. From the **Office** menu 🔘, click **Open**. Locate and then open **i01_Team_Report.docx**. From the **Office** menu 🔘, click **Save As**. Navigate to the location where you are saving your files, and then create a folder named Integrated Projects Chapter 1 Save the document as i01_Team_Report_Your_Name If necessary, display the formatting marks. Compare your screen with **Figure 1**.

3. On the **Insert tab**, in the **Header & Footer group**, click the **Footer** button, and then click **Edit Footer**. On the **Design tab**, in the **Insert group**, click the **Quick Parts** button, and then click **Field**. Under **Field names**, click **FileName**, and then click **OK**. In the **Close group**, click the **Close Header and Footer** button.

4. Press [Ctrl] + [End]. On the **Insert tab**, in the **Text group**, click the **Object button arrow**, and then click **Text from File**. See **Figure 2**.

   ■ **Continue to the next page to complete the skill**

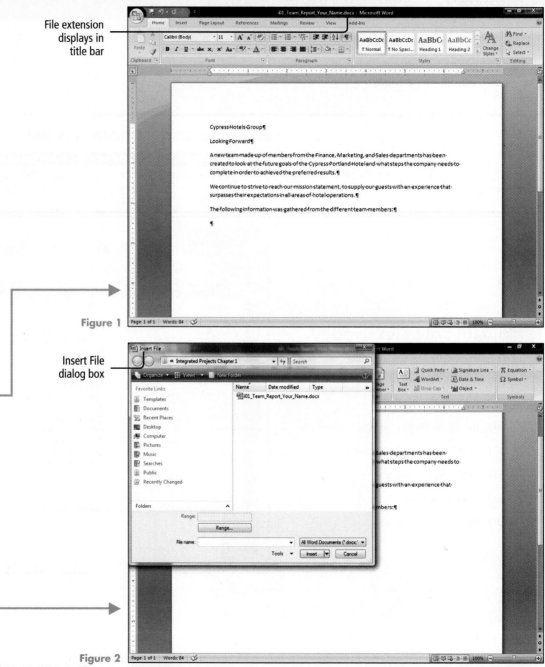

File extension displays in title bar

**Figure 1**

Insert File dialog box

**Figure 2**

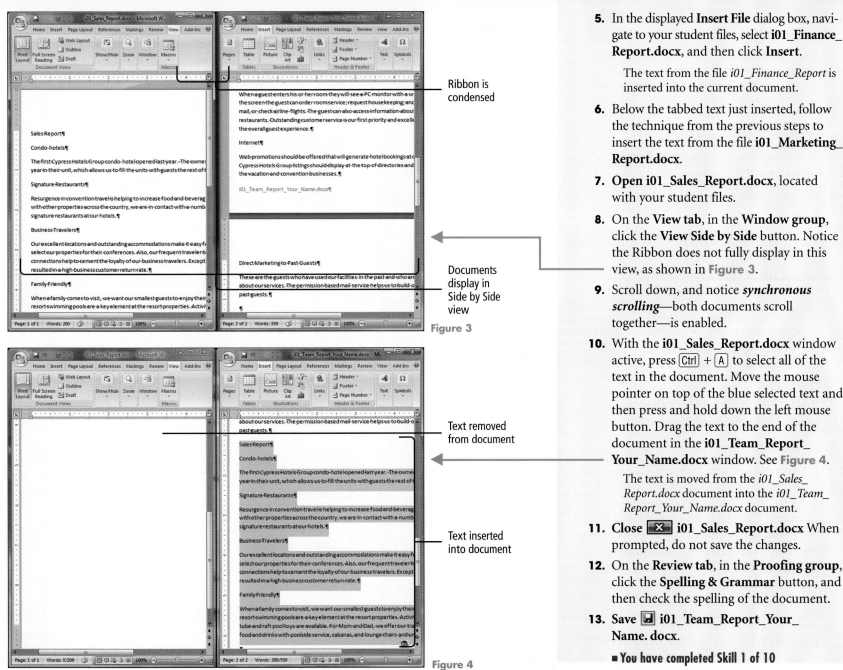

Ribbon is condensed

Documents display in Side by Side view

**Figure 3**

Text removed from document

Text inserted into document

**Figure 4**

5. In the displayed **Insert File** dialog box, navigate to your student files, select **i01_Finance_Report.docx**, and then click **Insert**.

   The text from the file *i01_Finance_Report* is inserted into the current document.

6. Below the tabbed text just inserted, follow the technique from the previous steps to insert the text from the file **i01_Marketing_Report.docx**.

7. **Open i01_Sales_Report.docx**, located with your student files.

8. On the **View tab**, in the **Window group**, click the **View Side by Side** button. Notice the Ribbon does not fully display in this view, as shown in **Figure 3**.

9. Scroll down, and notice *synchronous scrolling*—both documents scroll together—is enabled.

10. With the **i01_Sales_Report.docx** window active, press Ctrl + A to select all of the text in the document. Move the mouse pointer on top of the blue selected text and then press and hold down the left mouse button. Drag the text to the end of the document in the **i01_Team_Report_Your_Name.docx** window. See **Figure 4**.

    The text is moved from the *i01_Sales_Report.docx* document into the *i01_Team_Report_Your_Name.docx* document.

11. **Close** ⬛✖ **i01_Sales_Report.docx** When prompted, do not save the changes.

12. On the **Review tab**, in the **Proofing group**, click the **Spelling & Grammar** button, and then check the spelling of the document.

13. **Save** 🖫 **i01_Team_Report_Your_Name. docx**.

■ **You have completed Skill 1 of 10**

► Applying a heading style enables you to format all of that heading's text at one time.

► A **shortcut menu** is a menu that shows a list of commands relevant to a particular item and is displayed when you right-click an item.

1. Press ⌃Ctrl + End to move the insertion point to the end of the document.

2. Type Contact Us and then press Enter. Type Our team can be reached at (480) 555-0031.

3. Press ⌃Ctrl + Home to move the insertion point to the beginning of the document.

4. Select the first paragraph *Cypress Hotels Group*.

5. On the **Home tab**, in the **Styles group**, click the **Heading 1** button, and then compare with **Figure 1**.

6. Select the paragraph *Finance Report*. Press and hold ⌃Ctrl, and then select the paragraphs *Marketing Report*, *Sales Report*, and *Contact Us*.

7. Release ⌃Ctrl. With the four headings selected, click the **Heading 1** button.

8. Press ⌃Ctrl + Home to move the insertion point to the beginning of the document.

9. Using the same technique, select the paragraphs *Looking Forward*, *Condo-hotel Financing*, *Customer Service*, *Internet*, *Direct Marketing to Past Guests*, *Condo-hotels*, *Signature Restaurants*, *Business Travelers*, *Family Friendly*, and the last paragraph beginning *Our team can be reached*. In the **Styles group**, click the **Heading 2** button. Compare your screen with **Figure 2**.

■ Continue to the next page to complete the skill

Heading 1 button

Heading 1 style applied to paragraph

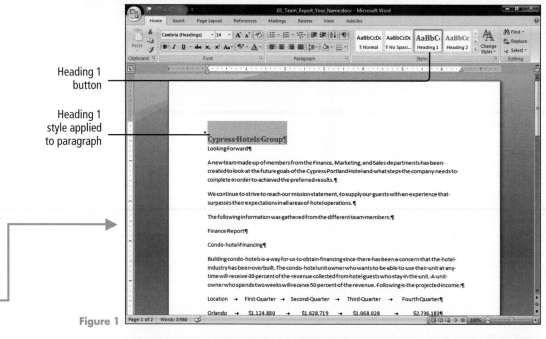

**Figure 1**

Heading 2 style applied

Heading 1 style applied

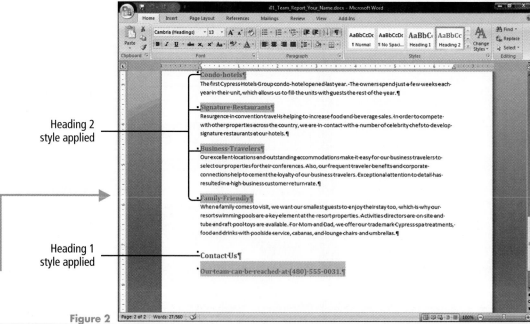

**Figure 2**

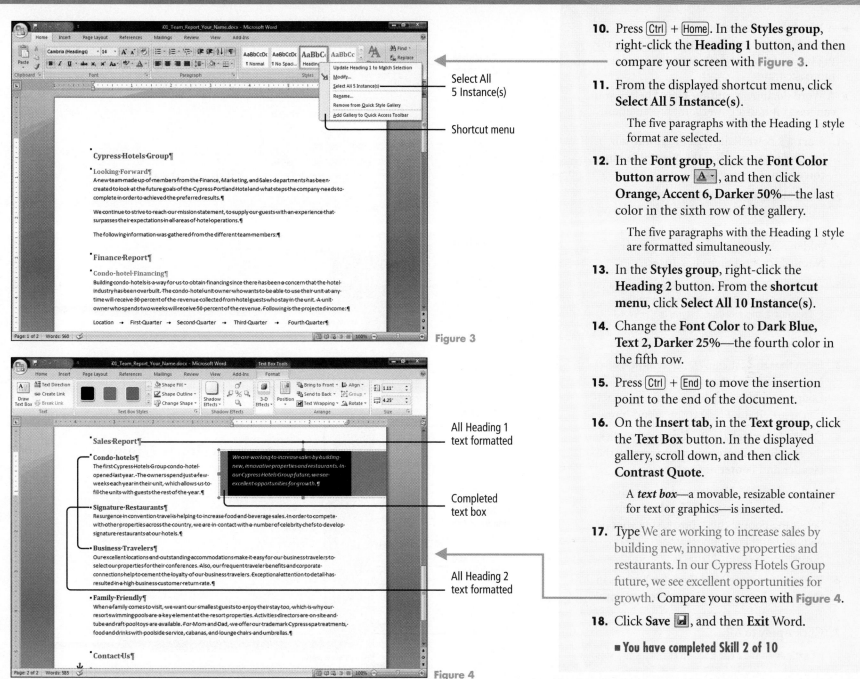

Figure 3

Select All
5 Instance(s)

Shortcut menu

All Heading 1
text formatted

Completed
text box

All Heading 2
text formatted

Figure 4

10. Press Ctrl + Home. In the **Styles group**, right-click the **Heading 1** button, and then compare your screen with **Figure 3**.

11. From the displayed shortcut menu, click **Select All 5 Instance(s)**.

    The five paragraphs with the Heading 1 style format are selected.

12. In the **Font group**, click the **Font Color button arrow** A ·, and then click **Orange, Accent 6, Darker 50%**—the last color in the sixth row of the gallery.

    The five paragraphs with the Heading 1 style are formatted simultaneously.

13. In the **Styles group**, right-click the **Heading 2** button. From the **shortcut menu**, click **Select All 10 Instance(s)**.

14. Change the **Font Color** to **Dark Blue, Text 2, Darker 25%**—the fourth color in the fifth row.

15. Press Ctrl + End to move the insertion point to the end of the document.

16. On the **Insert tab**, in the **Text group**, click the **Text Box** button. In the displayed gallery, scroll down, and then click **Contrast Quote**.

    A *text box*—a movable, resizable container for text or graphics—is inserted.

17. Type We are working to increase sales by building new, innovative properties and restaurants. In our Cypress Hotels Group future, we see excellent opportunities for growth. Compare your screen with **Figure 4**.

18. Click **Save** 🖫, and then **Exit** Word.

    ■ **You have completed Skill 2 of 10**

▶ A Word document can be inserted into a PowerPoint presentation. This avoids retyping the same data, which saves time and is more accurate.

▶ A Word document must be closed before you can insert it into a PowerPoint presentation.

1. **Start** 🎯 PowerPoint. On the **Home tab**, in the **Slides group**, click the **New Slide button arrow**. Compare with **Figure 1**.

2. Click **Slides from Outline**. In the displayed **Insert Outline** dialog box, navigate to your **Integrated Projects Chapter 1** folder. Select **i01_Team_Report_Your_Name.docx**, and then click **Insert**.

   A six-slide PowerPoint presentation is created from the paragraphs that were given the Heading 1 and Heading 2 styles in the Word document. Body text and objects such as the text box will not be inserted into the presentation.

3. From the **Office** menu 🗔, click **Save As**. Navigate to your **Integrated Projects Chapter 1** folder, and then **Save** the presentation as i01_Team_Presentation_Your_Name

4. On the **Insert tab**, in the **Text group**, click the **Header & Footer** button to display the **Header and Footer** dialog box.

5. In the displayed **Header and Footer** dialog box, click the **Notes and Handouts tab**. Select the **Footer** check box. Using your own first and last names, type i01_Team_Presentation_Your_Name

6. If necessary, clear any other check boxes in the dialog box. Compare your screen with **Figure 2**.

7. Click **Apply to All**.

   ■ **Continue to the next page to complete the skill**

New slide button arrow

Slides from Outline

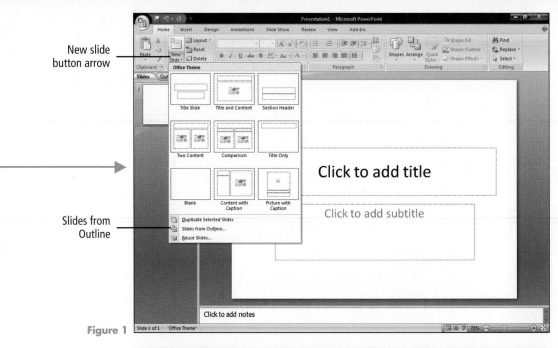

Click to add title

Click to add subtitle

**Figure 1**

Header and Footer dialog box

Notes and Handouts tab

Cleared check boxes

Footer text

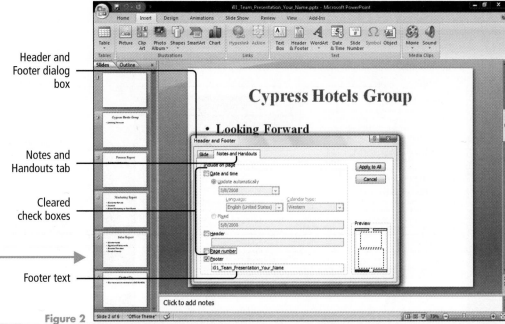

**Cypress Hotels Group**

• **Looking Forward**

**Figure 2**

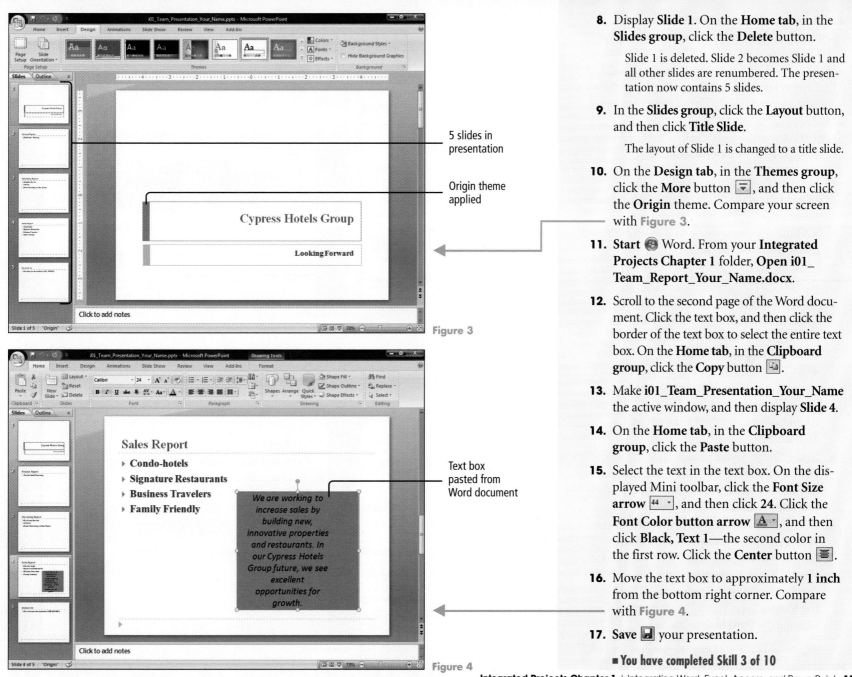

5 slides in presentation

Origin theme applied

**Figure 3**

Text box pasted from Word document

**Figure 4**

8. Display **Slide 1**. On the **Home tab**, in the **Slides group**, click the **Delete** button.

   Slide 1 is deleted. Slide 2 becomes Slide 1 and all other slides are renumbered. The presentation now contains 5 slides.

9. In the **Slides group**, click the **Layout** button, and then click **Title Slide**.

   The layout of Slide 1 is changed to a title slide.

10. On the **Design tab**, in the **Themes group**, click the **More** button ⬇, and then click the **Origin** theme. Compare your screen with **Figure 3**.

11. **Start** 🌐 Word. From your **Integrated Projects Chapter 1** folder, **Open i01_Team_Report_Your_Name.docx**.

12. Scroll to the second page of the Word document. Click the text box, and then click the border of the text box to select the entire text box. On the **Home tab**, in the **Clipboard group**, click the **Copy** button 📋.

13. Make **i01_Team_Presentation_Your_Name** the active window, and then display **Slide 4**.

14. On the **Home tab**, in the **Clipboard group**, click the **Paste** button.

15. Select the text in the text box. On the displayed Mini toolbar, click the **Font Size arrow** ⁴⁴ ▾, and then click **24**. Click the **Font Color button arrow** 🅰 ▾, and then click **Black, Text 1**—the second color in the first row. Click the **Center** button ≡.

16. Move the text box to approximately **1 inch** from the bottom right corner. Compare with **Figure 4**.

17. **Save** 💾 your presentation.

■ **You have completed Skill 3 of 10**

► *Shapes* are objects such as stars, banners, and callouts that can be inserted to emphasize a point.

► Shapes may have a yellow *adjustment handle*—a diamond-shaped handle used to adjust the appearance but not the size of most objects.

► Shapes can be modified with a *shape effect*—a pre-designed format that makes the shape look more professional.

1. In PowerPoint, display **Slide 5**. On the **Insert tab**, in the **Illustrations group**, click the **Shapes** button, and then click **Up Ribbon**—the first shape in the second row under **Stars and Banners**.

2. Click the middle of the slide to insert the shape.

3. On the **Format tab**, in the **Size group**, click the **Shape Height up spin arrow** 
   [⬆ 2" ⬍] to increase the height to **2.5**. Click in the **Shape Width** box, type 7.5 and then press Enter.

4. In the **Arrange group**, click the **Align** button, and then click **Align Center**. Click the **Align** button, and then click **Align Middle**. See Figure 1.

5. In the **Shape Styles group**, click the **Shape Fill** button, and then point to **Texture**. In the **Texture gallery**, click **Newsprint**—the first texture in the fourth row.

6. On the **Drawing Tools Format tab**, in the **WordArt Styles group**, click the **More** button [⬇], and then click **Fill - Accent 1, Plastic Bevel, Reflection**—the last style in the first row under **Applies to All Text in the Shape**. Type We value your input! Change the **Font Size** to **36**. See Figure 2.

■ **Continue to the next page to complete the skill**

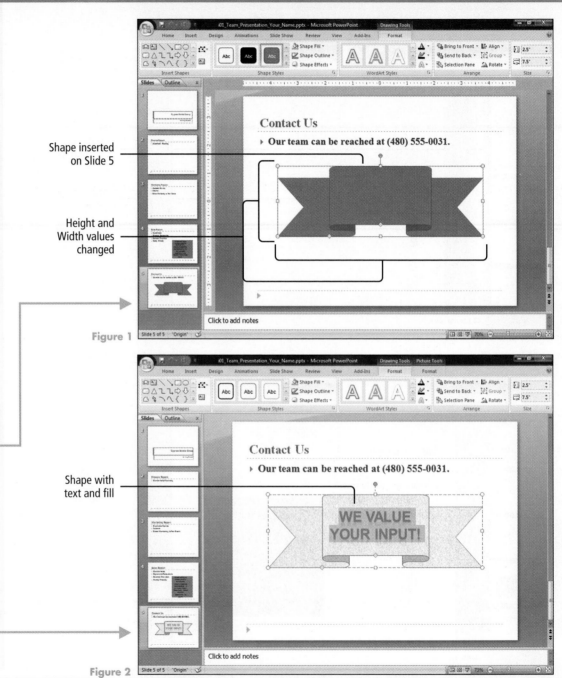

Shape inserted on Slide 5

Height and Width values changed

**Figure 1**

Shape with text and fill

**Figure 2**

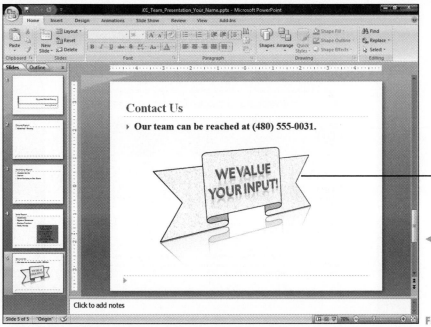

Shape with effects

Figure 3

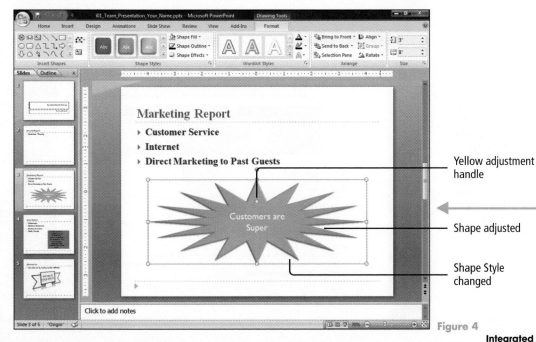

Yellow adjustment handle

Shape adjusted

Shape Style changed

Figure 4

7. In the **Shape Styles group**, click **Shape Outline**, and then click **Black, Text 1**.

8. Click **Shape Effects**, and then point to **3-D Rotation**. In the displayed **3-D Rotation gallery**, click **Perspective Contrasting Right**—the first effect in the third row under *Perspective*.

9. Click **Shape Effects**, and then point to **Reflection**. In the displayed **Reflection gallery**, click **Tight Reflection, touching**—the first effect in the first row under **Reflection Variations**. Click a blank area in the slide, and then compare your screen with **Figure 3**.

10. Display **Slide 3**. Using the same techniques, insert the shape **16-Point Star** in the middle of the slide.

11. Increase the height of the shape to **3"**, and then increase the width of the shape to **8"**. Move the shape to the lower middle part of the slide.

12. Type Customers are Super Select the text, and then change the **Font Size** to **24**.

13. Point at the yellow adjustment handle to display the  pointer. Drag the adjustment handle down approximately **1/2"**.

14. In the **Shapes Styles group**, click the **More** button ![more], and then click **Intense Effect - Accent 2**—the third shape in the sixth row. Compare your screen with **Figure 4**.

15. **Save** ![save] your presentation.

▪ **You have completed Skill 4 of 10**

► If you have a table of numbers in Word, you can copy and paste the numbers into Excel, and then generate formulas in the Excel workbook.

► Recall that formulas are equations that perform calculations on values.

1. Make **i01_Team_Report_Your_Name. docx** the active window.

2. On the first page, select the six lines of tabbed text.

3. On the **Insert tab**, in the **Tables group**, click the **Table** button, and then click **Convert Text to Table**. In the displayed **Convert Text to Table** dialog box, click **OK**, and then notice that the tabbed text is converted to a table as displayed in **Figure 1**.

4. On the **Design tab**, in the **Table Styles group**, click the **More** button ⮟. Select **Medium Shading 2 - Accent 1**—the second style in the fifth row under **Built-In**.

5. On the **Layout tab**, in the **Alignment group**, click the **Align Center** button ▤.

6. In the **Cell Size group**, click the **AutoFit** button, and then click **AutoFit Contents**.

7. In the **Table group**, click the **Properties** button. In the displayed **Table Properties** dialog box, under **Alignment**, click **Center**, and then click **OK**. Compare your screen with **Figure 2**.

   The cell contents are centered vertically and horizontally and the table is horizontally centered on the page.

8. With the table still selected, on the **Home tab**, in the **Clipboard group**, click the **Copy** button ▣.

   ■ **Continue to the next page to complete the skill** ▸

Tabbed text converted to a table

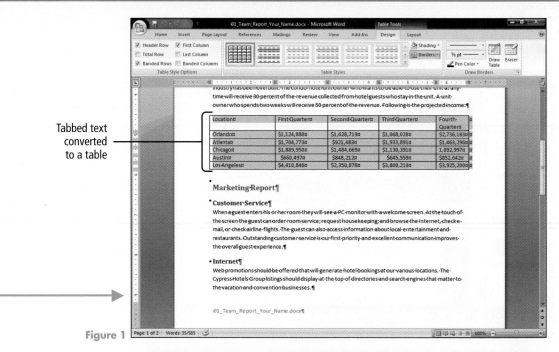

**Figure 1**

Table is centered horizontally on the page

Text is centered within each table cell

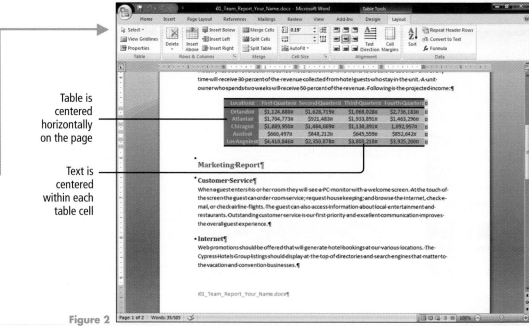

**Figure 2**

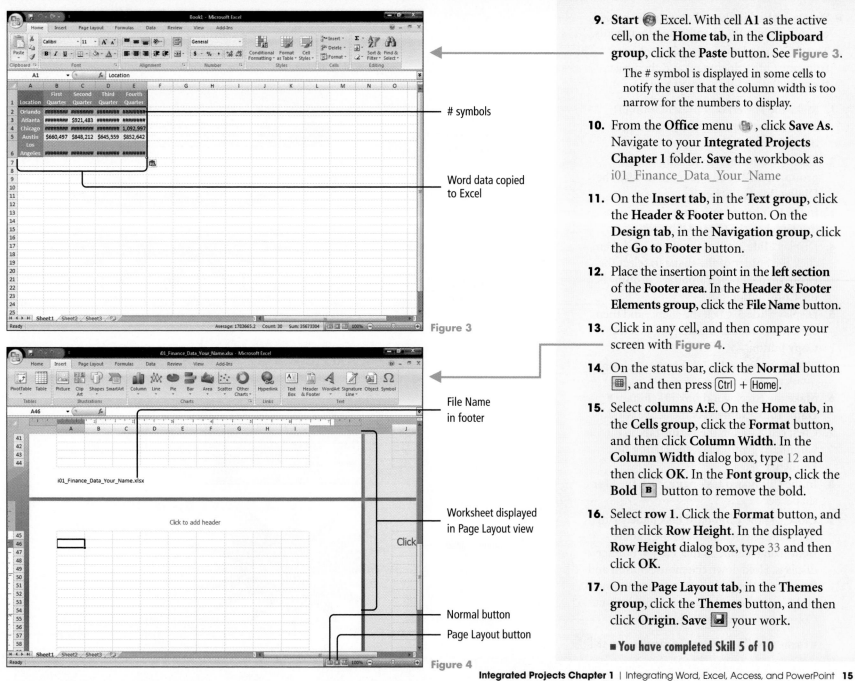

# symbols

Word data copied
to Excel

Figure 3

File Name
in footer

Worksheet displayed
in Page Layout view

Click

Normal button

Page Layout button

Figure 4

9. **Start** Excel. With cell **A1** as the active cell, on the **Home tab**, in the **Clipboard group**, click the **Paste** button. See **Figure 3**.

   The # symbol is displayed in some cells to notify the user that the column width is too narrow for the numbers to display.

10. From the **Office** menu , click **Save As**. Navigate to your **Integrated Projects Chapter 1** folder. **Save** the workbook as i01_Finance_Data_Your_Name

11. On the **Insert tab**, in the **Text group**, click the **Header & Footer** button. On the **Design tab**, in the **Navigation group**, click the **Go to Footer** button.

12. Place the insertion point in the **left section** of the **Footer area**. In the **Header & Footer Elements group**, click the **File Name** button.

13. Click in any cell, and then compare your screen with **Figure 4**.

14. On the status bar, click the **Normal** button , and then press Ctrl + Home.

15. Select **columns A:E**. On the **Home tab**, in the **Cells group**, click the **Format** button, and then click **Column Width**. In the **Column Width** dialog box, type 12 and then click **OK**. In the **Font group**, click the **Bold** B button to remove the bold.

16. Select **row 1**. Click the **Format** button, and then click **Row Height**. In the displayed **Row Height** dialog box, type 33 and then click **OK**.

17. On the **Page Layout tab**, in the **Themes group**, click the **Themes** button, and then click **Origin**. **Save** your work.

■ **You have completed Skill 5 of 10**

▶ Shapes created in PowerPoint can be copied and pasted into Word and Excel documents.

▶ The Office Clipboard can collect objects from any Office document and then paste them into other Office documents.

1. Make the PowerPoint presentation **i01_Team_Presentation_Your_Name.pptx** the active window.

2. On the **Home tab**, in the **Clipboard group**, in the lower right corner, click the **Dialog Box Launcher**.

3. In the **Clipboard task pane**, if any items display, click the **Clear All** button.

4. Display **Slide 3**. Click the shape, and then click the border of the shape to select the entire shape. In the **Clipboard group**, click the **Copy** button.

5. Display **Slide 5**. Click the shape, and then click the border of the shape. Click the **Copy** button.

   Both shapes are displayed in the Clipboard task pane.

6. Make the Excel workbook **i01_Finance_Data_Your_Name.xlsx** the active window.

7. Click cell **A10**. On the **Home tab**, in the **Clipboard group**, click the **Dialog Box Launcher**.

8. In the **Clipboard task pane**, click the **Star** shape. See **Figure 1**.

9. **Close** the **Clipboard task pane**. With the shape selected, point to the middle right sizing handle so that the pointer displays. Hold down the mouse button and drag left to the gridline between **columns F** and **G**, and then release the mouse button. Compare your screen with **Figure 2**.

   ▪ **Continue to the next page to complete the skill**

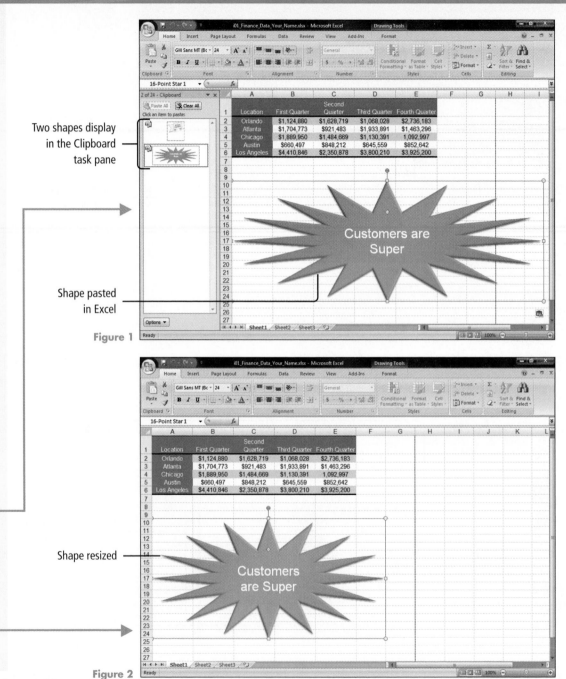

Two shapes display in the Clipboard task pane

Shape pasted in Excel

**Figure 1**

Shape resized

**Figure 2**

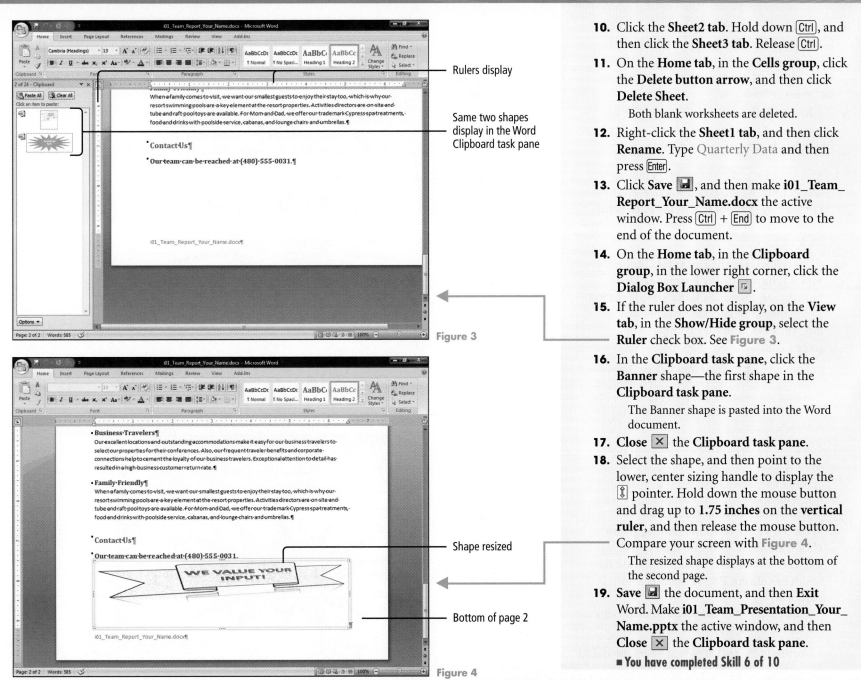

Rulers display

Same two shapes display in the Word Clipboard task pane

Figure 3

Shape resized

Bottom of page 2

Figure 4

**10.** Click the **Sheet2 tab**. Hold down Ctrl, and then click the **Sheet3 tab**. Release Ctrl.

**11.** On the **Home tab**, in the **Cells group**, click the **Delete button arrow**, and then click **Delete Sheet**.

Both blank worksheets are deleted.

**12.** Right-click the **Sheet1 tab**, and then click **Rename**. Type Quarterly Data and then press Enter.

**13.** Click **Save**, and then make **i01_Team_Report_Your_Name.docx** the active window. Press Ctrl + End to move to the end of the document.

**14.** On the **Home tab**, in the **Clipboard group**, in the lower right corner, click the **Dialog Box Launcher**.

**15.** If the ruler does not display, on the **View tab**, in the **Show/Hide group**, select the **Ruler** check box. See **Figure 3**.

**16.** In the **Clipboard task pane**, click the **Banner** shape—the first shape in the **Clipboard task pane**.

The Banner shape is pasted into the Word document.

**17.** **Close** the **Clipboard task pane**.

**18.** Select the shape, and then point to the lower, center sizing handle to display the pointer. Hold down the mouse button and drag up to **1.75 inches** on the **vertical ruler**, and then release the mouse button. Compare your screen with **Figure 4**.

The resized shape displays at the bottom of the second page.

**19.** **Save** the document, and then **Exit** Word. Make **i01_Team_Presentation_Your_Name.pptx** the active window, and then **Close** the **Clipboard task pane**.

■ **You have completed Skill 6 of 10**

► An Excel table enables you to format, sort, filter, and calculate a group of related data.

► *Criteria* are conditions that you specify to limit choices. A *filter* will hide rows that do not meet criteria.

► A *filter drop-down list* is a control that displays a list of filter options for each column in the header row of an Excel table.

1. Make the Excel workbook **i01_Finance_Data_Your_Name.xlsx** the active window. On the **Page Layout tab**, in the **Page Setup group**, click the **Margins** button, and then click **Narrow**.

2. Click cell **A1**. On the **Home tab**, in the **Styles group**, click the **Format as Table** button, and then click **Table Style Light 9**. In the displayed **Format As Table** dialog box, click **OK**, and then compare your screen with **Figure 1**.

   The range is converted into an *Excel table*— a series of rows and columns that contains related data that are managed independently from the data in other rows and columns on the worksheet.

3. Click cell **F1**, type Annual Total and then press Enter.

   *AutoExpansion* automatically includes an adjoining column in a table. Column F is incorporated into the Excel table.

4. With cell **F2** active, in the **Editing group**, click the **Sum** button, and then press Enter to create a calculated column. Increase the width of **column F** to **12**, and then compare with **Figure 2**.

   In an Excel table, a *calculated column* uses a single formula that adjusts for each row.

   ■ **Continue to the next page to complete the skill**

Filter drop down arrows

Excel table

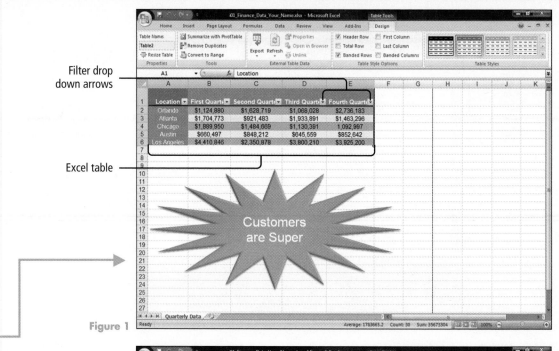

Figure 1

Calculated column

Formulas inserted in remaining rows

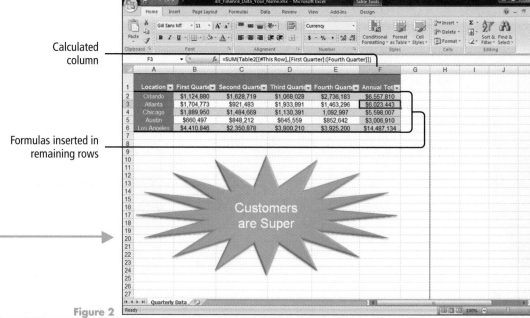

Figure 2

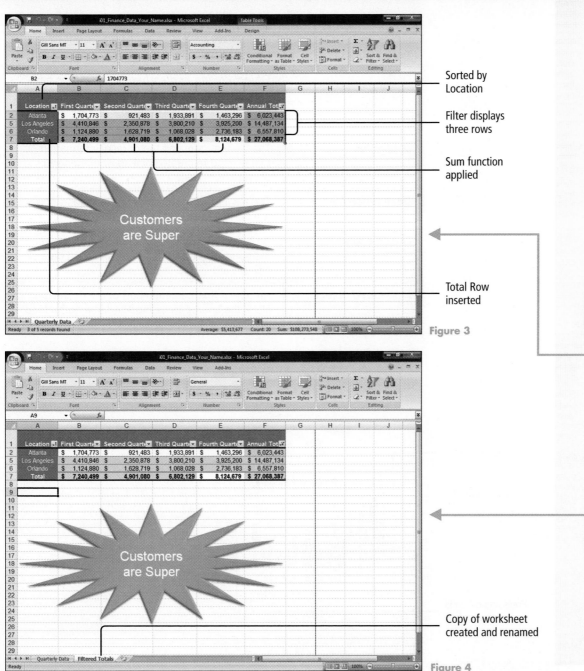

Sorted by
Location

Filter displays
three rows

Sum function
applied

Total Row
inserted

**Figure 3**

Copy of worksheet
created and renamed

**Figure 4**

5. On the **Design tab**, in the **Table Style Options group**, select the **Total Row** check box. Click cell **B7**, click its displayed **arrow** ▾, and then click **Sum**. Repeat this technique for cells **C7**, **D7**, and **E7**.

6. Select cells **B2:F7**. On the **Home tab**, in the **Styles group**, click the **Cell Styles** button, and then under **Number Format**, click **Currency [0]**.

7. In cell **A1**, click the **Filter arrow** ▾ to display the filter drop-down list. Click **Sort A to Z**.

   The rows are sorted in alphabetical order by location.

8. In cell **F1**, click the **Filter arrow** ▾. In the filter drop-down list, point to **Number Filters**, and then click **Greater Than**. In the displayed **Custom AutoFilter** dialog box, type 6000000 and then click **OK**. Compare your screen with **Figure 3**.

9. Right-click the **Quarterly Data sheet tab**, and then click **Move or Copy**. In the **Move or Copy** dialog box, click (**move to end**), select the **Create a copy** check box, and then click **OK**.

10. Right-click the **Quarterly Data(2) sheet tab**, and then click **Rename**. Type Filtered Totals and then press Enter. Click cell **A9**, and then compare your screen with **Figure 4**.

11. Click the **Quarterly Data sheet tab**. On the **Home tab**, in the **Editing group**, click the **Sort & Filter** button, and then click **Clear**.

12. Click the **Filtered Totals sheet tab**. Notice the filter is still applied on this worksheet.

13. **Save** 🖫 the workbook.

   ■ **You have completed Skill 7 of 10**

► Charts make it easy for users to see comparisons and trends in data.

► You can share information between files through linked or embedded objects.

1. An *external reference* creates a reference between objects in different files. Take a moment to examine common terms regarding external references, as described in the table in **Figure 1**.

2. Display the **Quarterly Data** worksheet, and then select cells **A1:E6**. On the **Insert tab**, in the **Charts group**, click the **Column** button. Under **Cylinder**, click **Clustered Cylinder**—the first type.

3. Move the chart below the shape so that its top left corner is in cell **A27**.

4. On the **Design tab**, in the **Data group**, click the **Switch Row/Column** button.

   The data series in the chart is switched. The quarter headings move to the horizontal axis and the location headings move to the legend.

5. On the **Layout tab**, in the **Labels group**, click the **Chart Title** button, and then click **Above Chart**. Type Projected Income and then press Enter. See **Figure 2**.

6. Click the chart border to select the chart. On the **Home tab**, in the **Clipboard group**, click the **Copy** button 📋.

7. Make the PowerPoint presentation **i01_Team_Presentation_Your_Name.pptx** the active window. Display **Slide 2**. On the **Home tab**, in the **Slides group**, click the **New Slide button arrow**, and then click **Blank**.

   A new blank slide, Slide 3, is inserted.

   ■ **Continue to the next page to complete the skill**

| External References | |
|---|---|
| **Type** | **Description** |
| ***OLE*** | ***Object linking and embedding (OLE)*** is an application-integration technology that shares information between programs through linked or embedded objects. |
| ***Source file*** | The file that contains the original information that is used to create a linked or embedded object. |
| ***Destination file*** | The file into which a linked or embedded object is inserted. |
| ***Linked object*** | An object that maintains a connection between the source and destination files. Linked data or objects are stored in the source file. |
| ***Embedded object*** | An object that becomes part of the destination file. If the source file is modified, the embedded object does not change. |

Figure 1

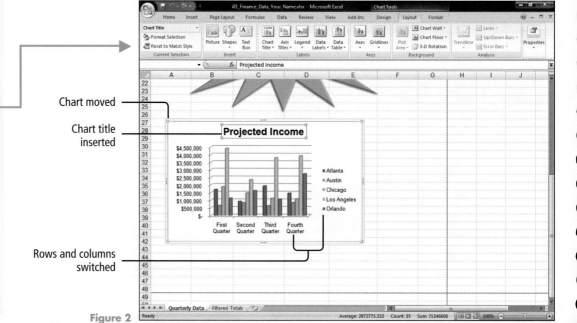

Chart moved

Chart title inserted

Rows and columns switched

Figure 2

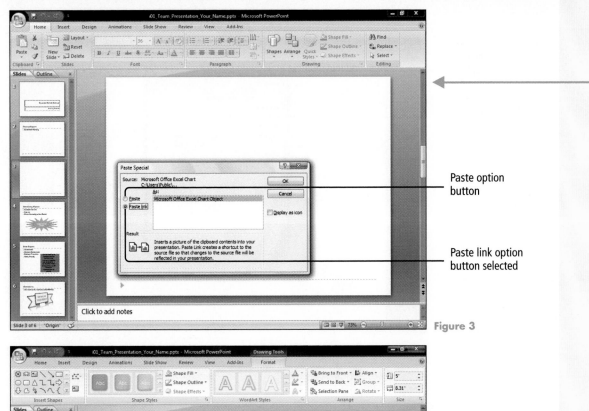

Paste option button

Paste link option button selected

Figure 3

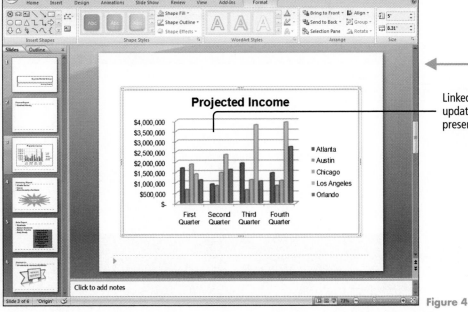

Linked chart updated in presentation

Figure 4

8. In the **Clipboard group**, click the **Paste button arrow**, and then click **Paste Special**. In the displayed **Paste Special** dialog box, click the **Paste link** option button. Compare your screen with Figure 3.

> The chart will be pasted as a *Microsoft Office Excel Chart Object*. Here, the *Paste* option button creates an embedded object. The *Paste link* option button creates a linked object.

9. In the **Paste Special** dialog box, click **OK**. On the **Format tab**, increase the **Shape Height** to 5".

10. In the **Arrange group**, click the **Align** button, and then click **Align Middle**. Click the **Align** button, and then click **Align Center**.

11. Make the source file **i01_Finance_Data_Your_Name.xlsx** the active window. Notice in the chart that Los Angeles had the highest projected income in the first quarter. Click cell **B5**, type 1410846 and then press Enter. Scroll down and notice that the Los Angeles first quarter column reflects the new value.

12. Make the destination file **i01_Team_Presentation_Your_Name.pptx** the active window. Compare your Los Angeles first column with Figure 4. If necessary, right-click the chart, and then from the displayed shortcut menu, click Update Link.

> The chart is a linked object. Changes made in the source file are reflected in the destination file.

13. **Save** the presentation, and then **Exit** PowerPoint. **Save** the workbook, and then **Exit** Excel.

■ **You have completed Skill 8 of 10**

► Word's mail merge feature creates customized letters, e-mail messages, envelopes, or labels.

► In Word's mail merge, the *main document* contains the text that remains constant. The *data source* contains the information—such as names and addresses—that changes with each letter or envelope.

1. **Start** ❂ Access. Under **Open Recent Database**, click **More**, navigate to your student data files, and then **Open i01_ Associates.accdb**.

2. **Open** the **Associates** table, view the records, and then **Exit** Access.

3. **Start** ❂ Word. **Save** the new document in your **Integrated Projects Chapter 1** folder as i01_Envelopes_Your_Name If necessary, display formatting marks.

4. Display the **Mailings tab**. In the **Start Mail Merge group**, click the **Start Mail Merge** button, and then click **Envelopes**. In the displayed **Envelope Options** dialog box, verify that the **Envelope size** is **Size 10**. See **Figure 1**.

5. In the **Envelope Options** dialog box, click **OK**. Notice that an envelope displays on your screen.

6. At the top left corner of the displayed envelope, type your first and last names, and then press [Enter]. Type 6803 N Navin Ave and then press [Enter]. Type Tampa, FL 33605 and then compare your screen with **Figure 2**.

7. On the **Mailings tab**, in the **Start Mail Merge group**, click the **Select Recipients** button, and then click **Use Existing List**.

■ **Continue to the next page to complete the skill**

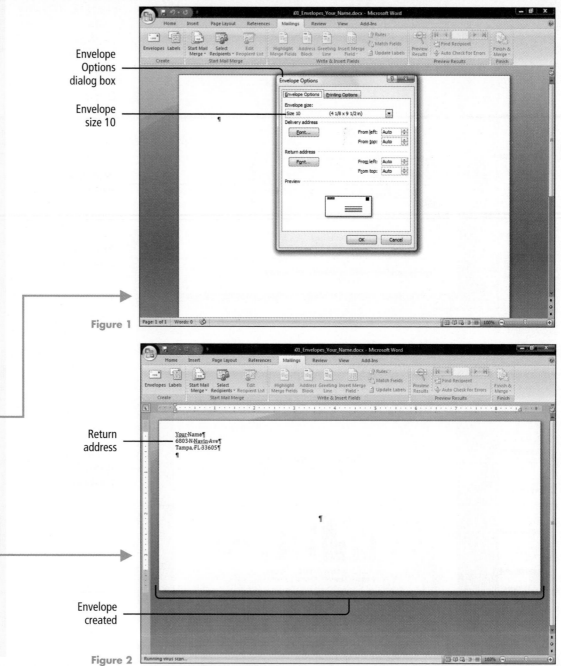

Envelope Options dialog box

Envelope size 10

**Figure 1**

Return address

Envelope created

**Figure 2**

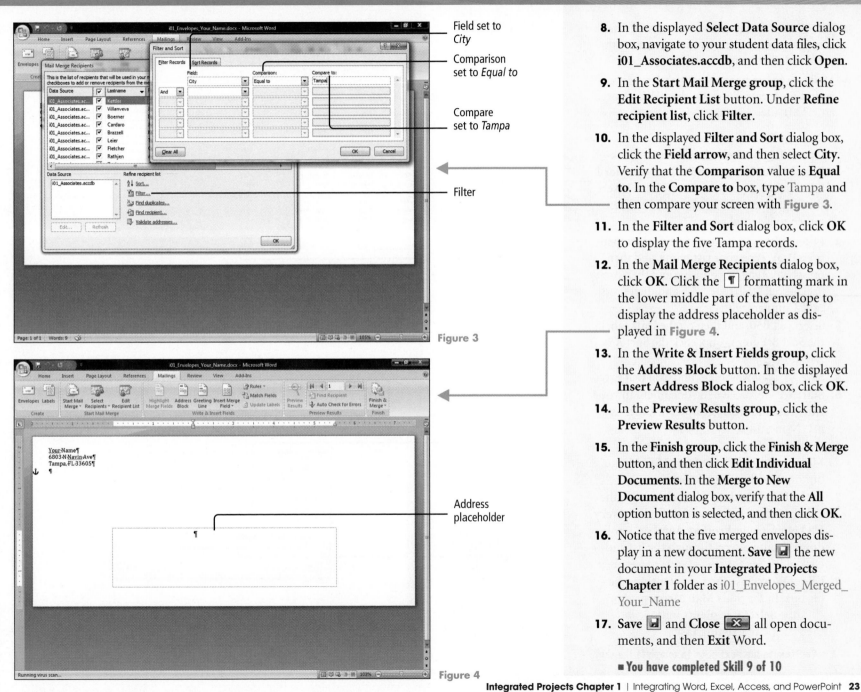

Figure 3

Field set to *City*

Comparison set to *Equal to*

Compare set to *Tampa*

Filter

Address placeholder

Figure 4

8. In the displayed **Select Data Source** dialog box, navigate to your student data files, click **i01_Associates.accdb**, and then click **Open**.

9. In the **Start Mail Merge group**, click the **Edit Recipient List** button. Under **Refine recipient list**, click **Filter**.

10. In the displayed **Filter and Sort** dialog box, click the **Field arrow**, and then select **City**. Verify that the **Comparison** value is **Equal to**. In the **Compare to** box, type Tampa and then compare your screen with **Figure 3**.

11. In the **Filter and Sort** dialog box, click **OK** to display the five Tampa records.

12. In the **Mail Merge Recipients** dialog box, click **OK**. Click the ¶ formatting mark in the lower middle part of the envelope to display the address placeholder as displayed in **Figure 4**.

13. In the **Write & Insert Fields group**, click the **Address Block** button. In the displayed **Insert Address Block** dialog box, click **OK**.

14. In the **Preview Results group**, click the **Preview Results** button.

15. In the **Finish group**, click the **Finish & Merge** button, and then click **Edit Individual Documents**. In the **Merge to New Document** dialog box, verify that the **All** option button is selected, and then click **OK**.

16. Notice that the five merged envelopes display in a new document. **Save** the new document in your **Integrated Projects Chapter 1** folder as i01_Envelopes_Merged_Your_Name

17. **Save** and **Close** all open documents, and then **Exit** Word.

■ **You have completed Skill 9 of 10**

► Word's mail merge feature can sort or filter records before the records are merged with the Word document.

► Mail merge can use a variety of data sources including Access, Excel, Outlook, Word, or an HTML file.

1. **Start** Excel. From your student files, **Open i01_Speakers.xlsx**, **Save** the workbook in your **Integrated Projects Chapter 1** folder as i01_Speakers_Your_Name **Insert** the file name in the left **Footer**, and then return to **Normal** view.

2. In cell **A50**, type your first name, and then press Tab. Type your last name, and then press Tab. Type Accounting and then press Tab. In cell **D50**, type 5775 and then press Enter. Compare with **Figure 1**.

3. Select cell **B50**, and then on the **Data tab**, in the **Sort & Filter group**, click the **Sort A to Z** button.

4. **Save** your workbook, and then **Exit** Excel.

5. **Start** Word. **Save** the document in your **Integrated Projects Chapter 1** folder as i01_Name_Tags_Your_Name

6. On the **Mailings tab**, in the **Start Mail Merge group**, click the **Start Mail Merge** button, and then click **Labels**.

7. In the **Label Options** dialog box, click the **Label vendors arrow**, and then click **Avery US Letter**. Under **Product number**, scroll down about halfway through the list and click **5095**. See **Figure 2**.

8. Click **OK** to close the **Label Options** dialog box. In the **Start Mail Merge group**, click the **Select Recipients** button, and then click **Use Existing List**.

■ Continue to the next page to complete the skill

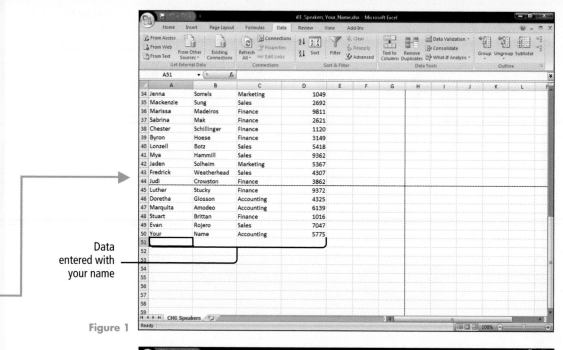

Data entered with your name

Figure 1

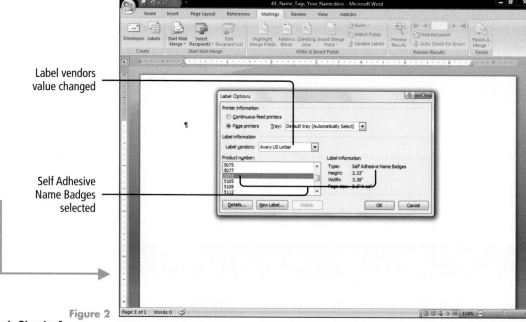

Label vendors value changed

Self Adhesive Name Badges selected

Figure 2

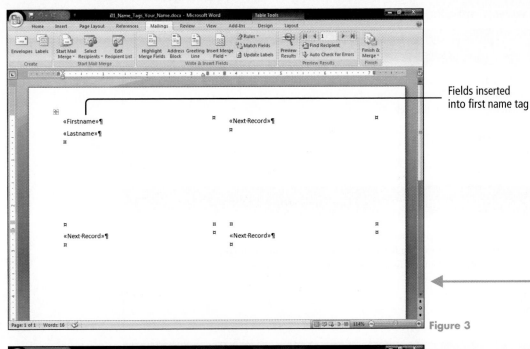

Fields inserted into first name tag

**Figure 3**

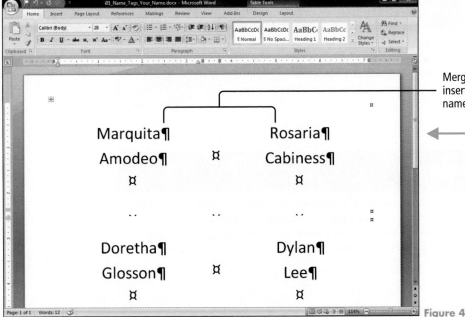

Merged fields inserted in all name tags

**Figure 4**

9. In the displayed **Select Data Source** dialog box, navigate to your **Integrated Projects Chapter 1** folder, and then open **i01_Speakers_Your_Name.xlsx**. In the **Select Table** dialog box, click **OK**.

10. Click the **Edit Recipient List** button, **Filter** the data to display the department **Accounting**, and then click **OK**. In the **Write & Insert Fields group**, click the **Insert Merge Field button arrow**, and then click **Firstname**. Press Enter. Click the **Insert Merge Field button arrow**, and then click **Lastname**. See **Figure 3**.

11. Above the first label, click the **Layout Selector** ⊞.On the Mini toolbar, change the **Font Size** to **28**.

12. On the **Layout tab**, in the **Alignment group**, click the **Align Center** button ▤.

13. On the **Mailings tab**, in the **Write & Insert Fields group**, click the **Update Labels** button. In the **Preview Results group**, click the **Preview Results** button to display all the merged name tags. See **Figure 4**.

14. In the **Finish group**, click the **Finish & Merge** button, and then click **Edit Individual Documents**. In the **Merge to New Document** dialog box, click **OK**.

15. On the **Home tab**, in the **Paragraph group**, click the **Show/Hide** button ¶ to turn off the formatting marks. **Save** the document in your **Integrated Projects Chapter 1** folder as i01_Accounting_Tags_Your_Name

16. **Save** 🖫 and **Close** ✖ all open documents, and then **Exit** Word.

17. Submit your files as directed.

**Done!** You have completed Skill 10 of 10 and your documents are complete!

# More Skills

The following More Skills are located at **www.prenhall.com/skills**

## More Skills (11) Insert Subtotals in Excel and Link Data to a Word Document

Excel can calculate summary statistics, such as totals or averages, by using the SUBTOTAL function. You can link data in Excel to a Word document. When the data in Excel are updated, the subtotals in the linked Word document will update.

In More Skills 11, you will open an Excel workbook, insert subtotals, and then link the data to a Word document. To begin, open your Internet browser, navigate to www.prenhall.com/skills, locate the name of your textbook, and then follow the instructions on the website.

## More Skills (12) Insert Slides from Another Presentation

PowerPoint slides can be duplicated in the same presentation, or slides can be added from a different presentation. Consistency between presentations is provided by reusing slides from different presentations.

In More Skills 12, you will open a presentation and duplicate slides. You will then reuse slides from a different presentation. To begin, open your Internet browser, navigate to www.prenhall.com/skills, locate the name of your textbook, and then follow the instructions on the website.

## More Skills (13) Move and Copy Excel Worksheets and Consolidate Data

An Excel worksheet can be moved or copied in the same workbook or to a different Excel workbook. The Move or Copy tool is used to organize worksheets from different workbooks into a single workbook.

In More Skills 13, you will open three Excel workbooks, and then copy the worksheets into one workbook. You will then create a summary worksheet to display the totals of the three copied worksheets. To begin, open your Internet browser, navigate to www.prenhall.com/skills, locate the name of your textbook, and then follow the instructions on the website.

## More Skills (14) Compare Shared Excel Workbooks

A shared workbook allows many users to view and make changes in the workbook at the same time. The Compare and Merge Workbooks feature can be used to compare the changes that have been made before you update the workbook.

In More Skills 14, you will open a shared workbook, add the Compare and Merge Workbooks icon to the Quick Access Toolbar, and then merge the workbooks. You will then accept and reject the changes. To begin, open your Internet browser, navigate to www.prenhall.com/skills, locate the name of your textbook, and then follow the instructions on the website.

# Key Terms

# Online Help Skills

1. **Start** your Web browser, for example Internet Explorer. In the **Address Bar**, type www.microsoft.com/word and then press [Enter] to display the **Word Home Page** for Microsoft Office Online.

2. In the upper left portion of the screen, click the text *Search Word 2007*, type set password and then press [Enter]. In the list of results, scroll down, and then click **Demo: Set a password to open or modify a workbook, document, or presentation.** Take a moment to read the information. Then, turn on your speakers or put on headphones, click **Play Demo**. The demo will begin as shown in Figure 1, and is only a few minutes in length.

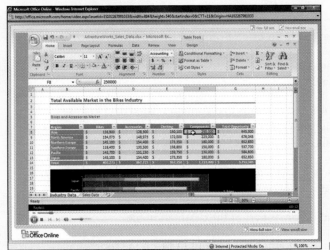

Figure 1

3. After you watch the demo, see if you can answer the following question: Why would you password protect a file?

# Matching

Match each term in the second column with its correct definition in the first column by writing the letter of the term on the blank line in front of the correct definition.

____ **1.** A set of characters added to the end of a file name that identifies the file type.

____ **2.** A list of commands relevant to a particular item that displays when the item is right-clicked.

____ **3.** A yellow diamond-shaped handle used to adjust the appearance but not the size of objects.

____ **4.** An object that can be inserted to emphasize a point.

____ **5.** The conditions you specify to limit which records are included in the result of a filter.

____ **6.** A range of rows and columns that contain related data that is managed independently from the data in other rows and columns on the worksheet.

____ **7.** A control that displays a list of filter and sort options for a column in an Excel table or Access datasheet.

____ **8.** An object that becomes part of the destination file.

____ **9.** An object that maintains a connection between the source and destination files.

____**10.** An application-integration technology that you can use to share information between programs.

**A** Adjustment handle

**B** Criteria

**C** Embedded object

**D** Excel table

**E** File extension

**F** Filter drop-down list

**G** Linked object

**H** OLE

**I** Shape

**J** Shortcut menu

# Fill in the Blank

Write the correct answer in the space provided.

1.  In Side by Side view in Word, when two documents scroll together it is called _____ scrolling.

2.  Shapes can be modified with a _____ _____—a predesigned format that makes a shape look more professional.

3.  In an Excel table, _____ automatically includes an adjoining column in a table.

4.  In an Excel table, a _____ _____ uses a single formula that adjusts for each row. It automatically expands to include additional rows so that the formula is immediately extended to those rows.

5.  A _____ will hide rows that do not meet specific criteria.

6.  The file that a linked or embedded object is inserted into is called a _____ file.

7.  A _____ object becomes part of the destination file.

8.  A _____ reference creates a reference between objects in different files.

9.  A file that contains the original information that is used to create a linked or embedded object is called a _____ file.

10. The part of the Word mail merge feature that contains the text that remains constant is called the _____ _____.

# Topics for Discussion

1.  In this chapter, you practiced inserting text and objects from one Office 2007 application into another. When might this be helpful to a team member?

2.  In this chapter, you created a calculated column in an Excel table. Can you explain why it is faster and more accurate to use a calculated column rather than typing a formula in each Excel row?

# Skill Check 1

## To complete these files, you will need the following files:

- **New blank Excel workbook**
- **i01_Restaurant_Memo.docx**
- **i01_Restaurant_Presentation.pptx**

## You will save your files as:

- **i01_Restaurant_Income_Your_Name.xlsx**
- **i01_Restaurant_Memo_Your_Name.docx**
- **i01_Restaurant_Presentation_Your_Name.pptx**

**Figure 1**

1. Locate and **Open** the Word document **i01_Restaurant_Memo**. **Save** the document in your **Integrated Projects Chapter 1** folder as i01_Restaurant_Memo_Your_Name and then add the file name to the footer.

2. Select the eight lines of tabbed text. On the **Insert tab**, in the **Tables group**, click the **Table** button. Click **Convert Text to Table**, and then click **OK**.

3. On the **Design tab**, in the **Table Styles group**, click the **More** button, and then click **Medium Shading 2 - Accent 4**—the fifth style in the fifth row.

4. On the **Layout tab**, in the **Cell Size group**, click the **AutoFit** button, and then click **AutoFit Contents**. In the **Table group**, click the **Properties** button. Under **Alignment**, click **Center**, and then click **OK**. Select the cells containing numbers. In the **Alignment group**, click the **Align Center Right** button. See **Figure 1**.

5. **Save** the Word document. Select the table, and then on the **Home tab**, in the **Clipboard group**, click **Copy**.

6. **Start** Excel. **Save** the workbook in your **Integrated Projects Chapter 1** folder as i01_Restaurant_Income_Your_Name and then add the file name to the left side of the footer. Click the **Normal** view button, and then press Ctrl + Home. On the **Home tab**, in the **Clipboard group**, click the **Paste** button.

7. In the **Styles group**, click the **Format As Table** button, and then click **Table Style Light 12**. In the **Format As Table** dialog box, click **OK**.

8. On the **Home tab**, in the **Cells group**, click the **Format** button, and then click **Row Height**. In the **Row Height** dialog box, type 20 and then click **OK**. See **Figure 2**.

9. Make cell **E1** the active cell. Type Totals and then press Enter.

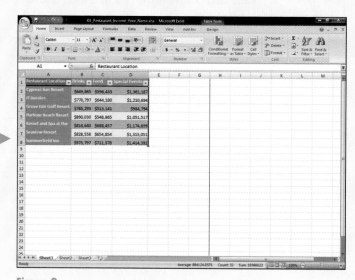

**Figure 2**

■ **Continue to the next page to complete Skill Check 1** ▶

**10.** Verify that cell **E2** is the active cell. In the **Editing group**, click the **Sum** button, and then press Enter.

**11.** Select **columns B:E**. In the **Cells group**, click the **Format** button, and then click **Column Width**. In the **Column Width** dialog box, type 14 and then click **OK**. **Save** the workbook.

**12.** **Open** the PowerPoint presentation **i01_Restaurant_Presentation**. **Save** the presentation in your **Integrated Projects Chapter 1** folder as i01_Restaurant_Presentation_ Your_Name and then type the file name in the **Notes and Handouts** footer.

**13.** On the **Design tab**, in the **Themes group**, click the **Module** theme. Display **Slide 3**. On the **Home tab**, in the **Slides group**, click the **New Slide button arrow**, and then click **Title Only**.

**14.** Make the Excel workbook **i01_Restaurant_Income_Your_Name** the active window. Select cells **A1:E8**, and then **Copy** the range of cells.

**15.** Make the presentation **i01_Restaurant_Presentation_Your_Name** the active window. If necessary, display Slide 4. On the **Home tab**, in the **Clipboard group**, click the **Paste** button.

**16.** On the **Layout tab**, in the **Table Size group**, increase the **Height** to **4.5"**, and then increase the **Width** to **8"**. In the **Arrange group**, click the **Align** button, and then click **Align Center**.

**17.** Select all the table cells. On the Mini toolbar, change the **Font Size** to **18**. Compare your screen with **Figure 3**.

**18.** On **Slide 4**, click the **Title** placeholder, and then type Restaurant Income by Location

**19.** Display **Slide 3**. On the **Insert tab**, in the **Illustrations group**, click the **Shapes** button, and then click **Vertical Scroll**—under **Stars and Banners**, the fifth shape in the second row. Click the right side of **Slide 3** to insert the shape.

**20.** On the **Format tab**, in the **Size group**, increase the **Height** to **4"**, and then increase the **Width** to **3"**. In the **Shape Styles group**, click the **Shape Effects** button. Point to **Shadow**, and then under **Perspective**, click **Perspective Diagonal Upper Left**.

**21.** Type Our special events depend on our customer loyalty and then select the text. On the Mini toolbar, change the **Font Size** to **28**. In the **WordArt Styles group**, click **Fill - Text 1, Inner Shadow**—the third style in the second row under Applies to Selected Text. Move the shape to the right side of the slide. Compare your screen with **Figure 4**.

**22.** **Save**, and then **Close** the files. Submit your files as directed.

**Done!** You have completed Skill Check 1

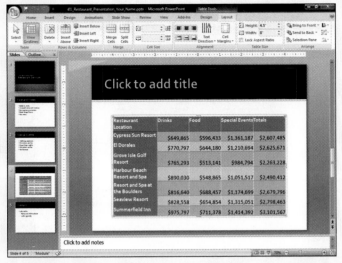

Figure 3

Figure 4

# Skill Check 2

## To complete these documents, you will need the following files:

- New blank Word document
- i01_Seminar.xlsx
- i01_Guests.accdb

## You will save your documents as:

- i01_Seminar_Tags_Your_Name.docx
- i01_Sales_Name_Tags_Your_Name.docx
- i01_Guest_Envelopes_Your_Name.docx
- i01_85017_Envelopes_Your_Name.docx

1. **Start** Word. **Save** the new document in your **Integrated Projects Chapter 1** folder as i01_Seminar_Tags_Your_Name

2. On the **Mailings tab**, in the **Start Mail Merge group**, click the **Start Mail Merge** button, and then click **Labels**. In the displayed **Labels Options** dialog box, click the **Label vendors arrow**, and then click **Avery US Letter**. Under **Product number**, click **5095**, and then click **OK**.

3. In the **Start Mail Merge group**, click the **Select Recipients** button, and then click **Use Existing List**. In the displayed **Select Data Source** dialog box, locate and **Open** the Excel workbook **i01_Seminar**, and then click **OK**.

4. In the **Start Mail Merge group**, click the **Edit Recipient List** button. In the **Mail Merge Recipients** dialog box, under **Refine recipient list**, click **Filter**. In the **Filter and Sort** dialog box, click the **Field arrow**, and then click **Department**. Verify that the **Comparison** box is **Equal to**. In the **Compare to** box, type Sales and then click **OK**. Compare your screen with **Figure 1**.

5. In the **Mail Merge Recipients** dialog box, click **OK**.

6. In the **Write & Insert Fields group**, click the **Insert Merge Field button arrow**, and then click **Firstname**. Type a space, click the **Insert Merge Field button arrow**, and then click **Lastname**. Above the first label, click the **Layout Selector**. On the Mini toolbar, change the **Font Size** to **26**. See **Figure 2**.

7. In the **Preview Results group**, click the **Preview Results** button.

▪ Continue to the next page to complete Skill Check 2 ➤

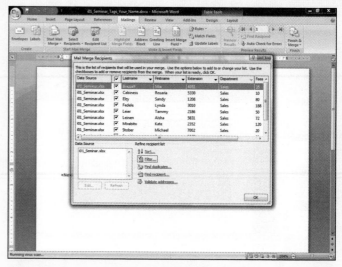

Figure 1

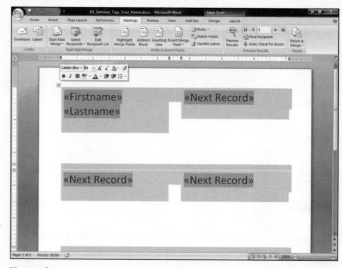

Figure 2

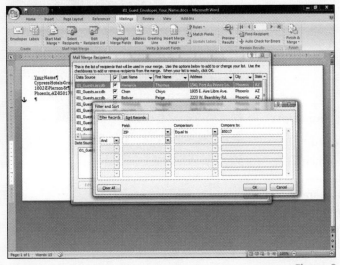

**Figure 3**

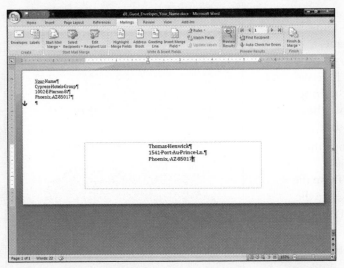

**Figure 4**

8. In the **Write & Insert Fields group**, click the **Update Labels** button. In the **Finish group**, click the **Finish & Merge** button, and then click **Edit Individual Documents**. In the **Merge to New Document** dialog box, click **OK**.

9. In the first name tag, delete the name, and then type your first and last names. **Save** the merged document in your **Integrated Projects Chapter 1** folder as i01_Sales_Name_Tags_Your_Name and then **Close** the document.

10. Make **i01_Seminar_Tags_Your_Name** the active window. Click **Save**, and then **Close** the document.

11. Create a new blank **Word** document. **Save** the new document in your **Integrated Projects Chapter 1** folder as i01_Guest_Envelopes_Your_Name

12. On the **Mailings tab**, in the **Start Mail Merge group**, click the **Start Mail Merge** button. Click **Envelopes**, and then click **OK**.

13. At the top left corner of the envelope, type Your Name and then press Enter. Type Cypress Hotels Group and then press Enter. Type 1002 E Pierson St and then press Enter. Type Phoenix, AZ 85017

14. Using the techniques from the previous steps, select recipients from an existing list using the Access database **i01_Guests**.

15. In the **Start Mail Merge group**, click **Edit Recipient List**. Under **Refine recipient list**, click **Filter**. Change the **Field** to **ZIP**, verify that **Comparison** is **Equal to**, and then in the **Compare to** box, type 85017 Compare your screen with **Figure 3**.

16. In the **Filter and Sort** dialog box, click **OK**, and then in the **Mail Merge Recipients** dialog box, click **OK**.

17. Click the lower middle part of the envelope to display an address placeholder. In the **Write & Insert Fields group**, click the **Address Block** button, and then click **OK**. In the **Preview Results group**, click the **Preview Results** button. Compare your screen with **Figure 4**.

18. In the **Finish group**, click the **Finish & Merge** button. Click **Edit Individual Documents**, and then click **OK**. **Save** the new document in your **Integrated Projects Chapter 1** folder as i01_85017_Envelopes_Your_Name and then **Close** the document.

19. Close **i01_Guest_Envelopes_Your_Name**. When prompted, **Save** the document. Submit your files as directed.

   **Done!** You have completed Skill Check 2

# Assess Your Skills 1

## To complete these files, you will need the following files:

- New blank PowerPoint presentation
- i01_Retirement.docx
- i01_Quote1.docx
- i01_Quote2.docx
- i01_Quote3.docx
- i01_Quote4.docx

## You will save your files as:

- i01_Retirement_Your_Name.docx
- i01_Retirement_Presentation_Your_Name.pptx

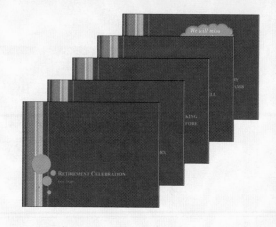

1. **Start** Word, and then **Open i01_Retirement**. **Save** the file in your **Integrated Projects Chapter 1** folder as i01_Retirement_Your_Name

2. In the second paragraph, replace the text *Your Name* with your own first and last names.

3. At the end of the document, insert the file **i01_Quote1**, and then insert the file **i01_Quote2**.

4. Open **i01_Quote3**. **Copy** and **Paste** the text from **i01_Quote3** to the end of the **i01_Retirement_Your_Name** document. **Close i01_Quote3**.

5. Open **i01 Quote4**. Move the text from the **i01_Quote4** file to the end of the **i01_Retirement_Your_Name** document. **Close i01_Quote4**. If prompted, do not save the changes.

6. Apply the **Heading 1** style to the paragraph *Retirement Celebration*, and then to the four quotations.

7. Select *Your Name* and the four paragraphs beginning *Submitted by*. Apply the **Heading 2** style.

8. Select all five instances of the **Heading 1** format, and then change the font color to **Orange, Accent 6**—the last color in the first row. Select all instances of the **Heading 2** format, and then change the font color to **Blue, Accent 1**—the fifth color in the first row.

9. **Save** your document, and then **Exit** Word.

10. **Start** PowerPoint. Insert the Word document **i01_Retirement_Your_Name**. **Save** the presentation in your **Integrated Projects Chapter 1** folder as i01_Retirement_Presentation_Your_Name In the **Notes and Handouts** footer, type the file name, and then click **Apply to All** handouts.

11. Apply the **Oriel** theme, and then delete **Slide 1**. Change the layout of all slides to **Section Header**.

12. On **Slide 5**, insert the shape **Cloud**—found under **Basic Shapes**. Increase the **Shape Height** to 2" and the **Shape Width** to 4". Add the **Bevel** Shape Effect, **Soft Round**. Type We will miss you in the office! Change the **Font Size** to **28**, and then apply **Italic**. Move the shape to the top right corner of the slide.

13. **Save** your presentation, and then **Copy** the shape. **Open** your Word document **i01_Retirement_Your_Name**, and then **Paste** the shape at the end of the document. Resize the shape to fill the blank area at the bottom of Page 1. Apply the **Oriel** theme.

14. Compare your completed documents with **Figure 1**. **Save** your files, and then submit your files as directed.

**Done!** You have completed Assess Your Skills 1

Figure 1

**MEMO**

TO: Wyatt Lebedev, Human Resources Representative

FROM: Jorge Brouhard, Sales Manager

DATE: November 29, 2010

RE: Winners of the Monthly commission prizes

We have received the sales numbers for October and are pleased to announce we have more winners this month than in any previous month. The Human Resources department has my authorization to issue a 3% commission check to the following list of Sales Representatives:

| Firstname | Lastname | Location | Sales | Commissions |
|---|---|---|---|---|
| Thomas | Torrex | Cypress Sun Resort | $ 79,588 | $ 2,388 |
| Sonya | Alire | Cypress Sun Resort | $ 99,063 | $ 2,972 |
| Kelly | McKennon | Cypress Sun Resort | $ 80,044 | $ 2,401 |
| Rosaria | Cabiness | El Dorales | $ 88,173 | $ 2,645 |
| Paul | Vandeveer | El Dorales | $ 90,572 | $ 2,717 |
| Timothy | Dominik | Grove Isle Golf Resort | $ 95,918 | $ 2,878 |
| Alaina | Wail | Grove Isle Golf Resort | $ 94,676 | $ 2,840 |
| Miranda | Hevey | Grove Isle Golf Resort | $ 81,645 | $ 2,449 |
| Tammy | Leier | Harbour Beach Resort and Spa | $ 75,174 | $ 2,255 |
| Jon | Yeater | Harbour Beach Resort and Spa | $ 81,269 | $ 2,438 |
| Rene | Hoots | Resort and Spa at the Boulders | $ 79,618 | $ 2,389 |
| Evan | Simson | Resort and Spa at the Boulders | $ 82,622 | $ 2,479 |
| Mackenzie | Sung | Seaview Resort | $ 77,538 | $ 2,326 |
| Kent | Schoenberger | Seaview Resort | $ 77,209 | $ 2,316 |
| LeeAnn | Kim | Seaview Resort | $ 97,911 | $ 2,937 |
| Denice | Faeth | Seaview Resort | $ 81,997 | $ 2,460 |
| Mia | Brazzell | Summerfield Inn | $ 76,756 | $ 2,303 |
| Carter | Tsui | Summerfield Inn | $ 94,877 | $ 2,846 |
| Sabrina | Mak | Summerfield Inn | $ 96,526 | $ 2,896 |
| Rhea | Hokama | Summerfield Inn | $ 93,579 | $ 2,807 |
| Fredrick | Clune | Summerfield Inn | $ 92,166 | $ 2,765 |
| Bryan | Vales | Summerfield Inn | $ 98,169 | $ 2,945 |
| Breanna | Everhart | Summerfield Inn | $ 95,419 | $ 2,863 |
| Total | | | $ 2,010,508 | $ 60,315 |

i01_Commissions_Report_Your_Name.docx

| Firstname | Lastname | Location | Sales | Commissions |
|---|---|---|---|---|
| Thomas | Torrex | Cypress Sun Resort | $ 79,588 | $ 2,388 |
| Sonya | Alire | Cypress Sun Resort | $ 99,063 | $ 2,972 |
| Kelly | McKennon | Cypress Sun Resort | $ 80,044 | $ 2,401 |
| Rosaria | Cabiness | El Dorales | $ 88,173 | $ 2,645 |
| Paul | Vandeveer | El Dorales | $ 90,572 | $ 2,717 |
| Timothy | Dominik | Grove Isle Golf Resort | $ 95,918 | $ 2,878 |
| Alaina | Wail | Grove Isle Golf Resort | $ 94,676 | $ 2,840 |
| Miranda | Hevey | Grove Isle Golf Resort | $ 81,645 | $ 2,449 |
| Tammy | Leier | Harbour Beach Resort and Spa | $ 75,174 | $ 2,255 |
| Jon | Yeater | Harbour Beach Resort and Spa | $ 81,260 | $ 2,438 |
| Rene | Hoots | Resort and Spa at the Boulders | $ 79,618 | $ 2,389 |
| Evan | Simson | Resort and Spa at the Boulders | $ 82,622 | $ 2,479 |
| Mackenzie | Sung | Seaview Resort | $ 77,538 | $ 2,326 |
| Kent | Schoenberger | Seaview Resort | $ 77,209 | $ 2,316 |
| LeeAnn | Kim | Seaview Resort | $ 97,911 | $ 2,937 |
| Denice | Faeth | Seaview Resort | $ 81,997 | $ 2,460 |
| Mia | Brazzell | Summerfield Inn | $ 76,756 | $ 2,303 |
| Carter | Tsui | Summerfield Inn | $ 94,877 | $ 2,846 |
| Sabrina | Mak | Summerfield Inn | $ 96,526 | $ 2,896 |
| Rhea | Hokama | Summerfield Inn | $ 93,579 | $ 2,807 |
| Fredrick | Clune | Summerfield Inn | $ 92,166 | $ 2,765 |
| Bryan | Vales | Summerfield Inn | $ 98,169 | $ 2,945 |
| Breanna | Everhart | Summerfield Inn | $ 95,419 | $ 2,863 |
| Total | | | $ 2,010,508 | 60,315 |

i01_Commissions_Your_Name.xlsx

**Figure 1**

# Assess Your Skills 2

## To complete these files, you will need the following files:

- i01_Commissions.xlsx
- i01_Commissions_Report.docx

## You will save your files as:

- i01_Commissions_Your_Name.xlsx
- i01_Commissions_Report_Your_Name.docx

1. **Start** Excel, and then **Open i01_Commissions**. **Save** the file in your **Integrated Projects Chapter 1** folder as i01_Commissions_Your_Name Add the file name to the left **footer**, and then return to Normal view.

2. Click cell **A2**. Format the range as an Excel table using the table style **Table Style Medium 7**.

3. In cell **E1**, type Commissions **AutoFit** the column widths of **columns A:E**.

4. In cell **E2**, enter the formula =D2*3% and then format the numbers in **column E** with the Cell Style **Currency [0]**.

5. Sort the **Location column** in ascending order. Filter the **Sales column** to display numbers greater than **75000**, and then insert a **Total Row**. In **column D**—the Sales column—on the **Total row**, insert the **SUM** function. If necessary, widen column D to display the total.

6. Create a copy of the **October Sales** worksheet. **Rename** the worksheet **October Sales(2)** to October Prize Winners

7. On the **October Sales** worksheet, remove the filter, and then **Save** the workbook.

8. **Start** Word, and then **Open i01_Commissions_Report**. **Save** the file in your **Integrated Projects Chapter 1** folder as i01_Commissions_Report_Your_Name and then add the file name to the footer.

9. Make the Excel workbook **i01_Commissions_Your_Name** the active window. Select the **October Prize Winners** worksheet, and then copy the filtered data in cells **A1:E118**.

10. Make the Word document **i01_Commissions_Report_Your_Name** the active window. Move to the end of the document, and then **Paste** the copied Excel data.

11. Select the table, and then apply the **AutoFit Contents** command.

12. Compare your completed documents with **Figure 1**. **Save** your Word document, and then **Exit** Word. **Exit** Excel. Submit your files as directed.

**Done!** You have completed Assess Your Skills 2

# Assess Your Skills 3

## To complete these files, you will need the following files:

- New blank Word document
- i01_Premier_Customers.accdb

## You will save your files as:

- i01_Premier_Envelopes_Your_Name.docx
- i01_Premier_Customers_Your_Name.accdb
- i01_MA_Envelopes_Your_Name.docx

1. **Start** Access. Navigate to your student data files. Select **i01_Premier_Customers**, and then click the **Open** button. **Save** the database as an **Access 2007 Database** in your **Integrated Projects Chapter 1** folder as i01_Premier_Customers_Your_Name

2. **Open** the **Premier Customers** table. In the first record, change *Your* and *Name* to your own first and last names. **Close** the table, and then **Exit** Access.

3. **Start** Word. **Save** the new document in your **Integrated Projects Chapter 1** folder as i01_Premier_Envelopes_Your_Name

4. Start a Mail Merge document for **Envelopes**. Use the **Size 10** envelope. In the top left corner of the envelope, type Cypress Hotels Group and then press [Enter]. Type 33 Herman Ave and then press [Enter]. Type Concord, MA 01742

5. **Select Recipients** using the existing list in the Access file **i01_Premier_Customers_Your_Name**.

6. **Filter** the recipients to display the three recipients from the **State** of MA

7. In the address placeholder, insert the **Address Block**, and then **Preview Results**.

8. **Finish & Merge** the document, and then **Save** the new document in your **Integrated Projects Chapter 1** folder as i01_MA_Envelopes_Your_Name

9. Compare your merged envelopes with **Figure 1**. **Save** your document, and then submit as directed.

**Figure 1**

**Done!** You have completed Assess Your Skills 3

# Assess Your Skills 4

**To complete these files, you will need the following files:**

- New blank Word document
- i01_Attendees.xlsx

**You will save your files as:**

- i01_Attendee_Tags_Your_Name.docx
- i01_Attendees_Your_Name.xlsx
- i01_Attendee_Tags_Merged_Your_Name.docx

**Figure 1**

1. **Start** Excel, and then **Open i01_Attendees**. **Save** the file in your **Integrated Projects Chapter 1** folder as i01_Attendees_Your_Name and then add the file name to the left footer.

2. Type the following data in row 17:

   | | |
   |---|---|
   | **Firstname** | Your first name |
   | **Lastname** | Your last name |
   | **Location** | Seaview Resort |
   | **Department** | Finance |

3. **Sort** the data in ascending order by the **Lastname column**.

4. **Save** the workbook, and then **Exit** Excel.

5. **Start** Word. **Save** the new document in your **Integrated Projects Chapter 1** folder as i01_Attendee_Tags_Your_Name

6. **Start Mail Merge** and select **Labels**. Select the Label vendor **Avery US Letter**, and then select the Product number **5095**.

7. **Select Recipients** for the mail merge using the Excel workbook **i01_Attendees_Your_**

Name and the worksheet **Conference Attendees**.

8. Insert the merge field **Firstname**. Type a space, and then insert the merge field **Lastname**. On the next line, insert the merge field **Location**. On the third line, insert the merge field **Department**. Format the **Firstname** and **Lastname** fields with the **Font Size 18**. Format the **Location** and **Department** fields with the **Font Size 14**.

9. **Update the Labels**, and then **Preview Results**.

10. Finish and merge the document to a new document, and then **Save** the file in your **Integrated Projects Chapter 1** folder as i01_Attendee_Tags_Merged_Your_Name

11. Compare your completed documents with **Figure 1**. **Save** your documents, and then **Exit** Word. Submit your files as directed.

   **Done!** You have completed Assess Your Skills 4

# More Integrated Projects for Word, Excel, Access, and PowerPoint

▶ Each Microsoft Office application has different strengths. Exporting data from one application to another enables you to use the strengths of each application without having to retype the data.

▶ Shared data can be linked or embedded, depending on the final use for the data.

## Your starting screen will look like this:

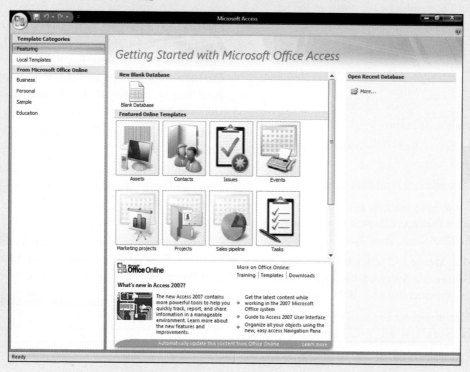

## SKILLS

### At the end of this chapter, you will be able to:

**Skill 1** Create an Access Append Query

**Skill 2** Export Data from Access into Excel

**Skill 3** Create an Excel PivotTable Report

**Skill 4** Create External References Between Excel Workbooks

**Skill 5** Insert a SmartArt Organization Chart into PowerPoint

**Skill 6** Insert an Excel PivotTable into PowerPoint

**Skill 7** Insert a PowerPoint Outline in Word and Create a Cover Page and Table of Contents

**Skill 8** Link and Embed Data from Excel into Word

**Skill 9** Export Data from Access to an RTF File and Insert the File into Word

**Skill 10** Insert Objects from PowerPoint into Word

### MORE SKILLS

**More Skills 11** Create an Excel PivotChart and Link the PivotChart to Word

**More Skills 12** Create a Hyperlink between PowerPoint, Word, and Excel Files

**More Skills 13** Insert a Total Row in an Excel Table and Link the Table to PowerPoint

**More Skills 14** Compare Word Documents

## Outcome

Using the skills listed to the left will enable you to create documents like this:

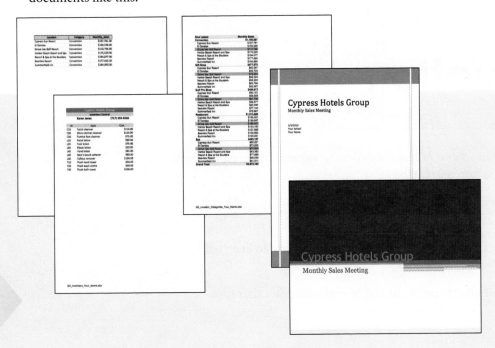

## You will save these files as:

i02_Convention_Sales_Your_Name.docx

i02_Convention_Sales_Your_Name.rtf

i02_Golf_Isle_Sales_Your_Name.accdb

i02_Inventory_Your_Name.xlsx

i02_Location_Categories_Your_Name.xlsx

i02_Location_Sales_Your_Name.accdb

i02_Meeting_Notes_Your_Name.docx

i02_Meeting_Your_Name.rtf

i02_Sales_Meeting_Your_Name.pptx

In this chapter, you will create files for the Cypress Hotels Group, which has large hotels located in major vacation and business destinations in North America.

# Introduction

- ▸ When data are stored in several Access databases, an append query enables you to combine all the data into one database.

- ▸ Excel provides a PivotTable report tool. Exporting data from Access into Excel enables you to create PivotTable reports for Access data.

- ▸ External references in Excel are useful when it is not practical to keep worksheets together in the same workbook.

- ▸ Once created, data and objects can be linked or embedded in other files.

**Time to complete all
10 skills - 60 minutes**

## Student data files needed
for this chapter:

- i02_Golf_Isle_Sales.accdb
- i02_Inventory.xlsx
- i02_Location_Sales.accdb
- i02_Meeting_Notes.docx
- i02_Sales_Meeting.pptx

## Find your student data files here:
You can find the files listed to the left by navigating through the student CD as shown below.

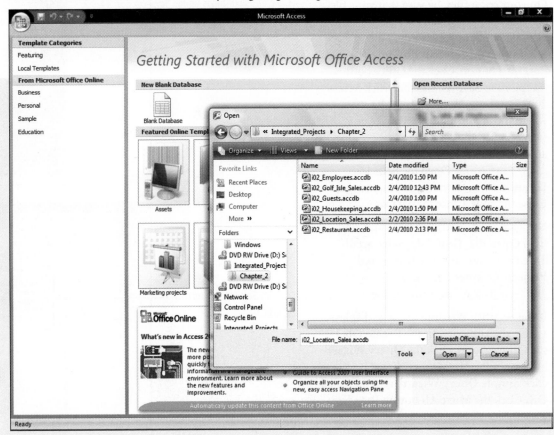

▶ An *append query* is a query that adds records to a destination table.

▶ In an append query, the data types in the source table must be compatible with the data types in the destination table.

▶ The Undo button will not remove records added by an append query.

1. On your computer, be sure that your file extensions display. **Start** 🔵 **Access.** Navigate to your student data files. Select **i02_Location_Sales.accdb**, and then click the **Open** button. Click the **Office** button 🔳, point to **Save As**, and then click **Access 2007 Database**. Navigate to the location where you are saving your files, create a folder named Integrated Projects Chapter 2 and then **Save** the database as i02_Location_ Sales_Your_Name **Open** the **Sales by Location** table, view the records, and then **Close** the table. **Close** the database.

2. Navigate to your student data files, and then **Open i02_Golf_Isle_Sales.accdb.** **Save** the database in the **Integrated Projects Chapter 2** folder as i02_Golf_Isle_Sales_Your_Name

3. If the Security Warning message displays, enable the content. On the **Create tab**, in the **Other group**, click the **Query Wizard** button. In the **New Query** dialog box, click **Simple Query Wizard**, and then click **OK**. Click the **Move All** button ⏩. See **Figure 1**.

4. Click **Finish**, and then see **Figure 2**.

   ◼ Continue to the next page to complete the skill ▶

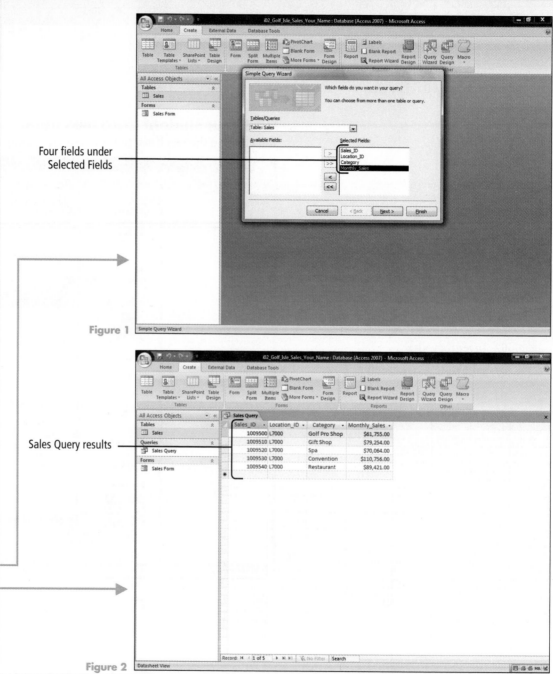

Four fields under Selected Fields

**Figure 1** Simple Query Wizard

Sales Query results

**Figure 2** Datasheet View

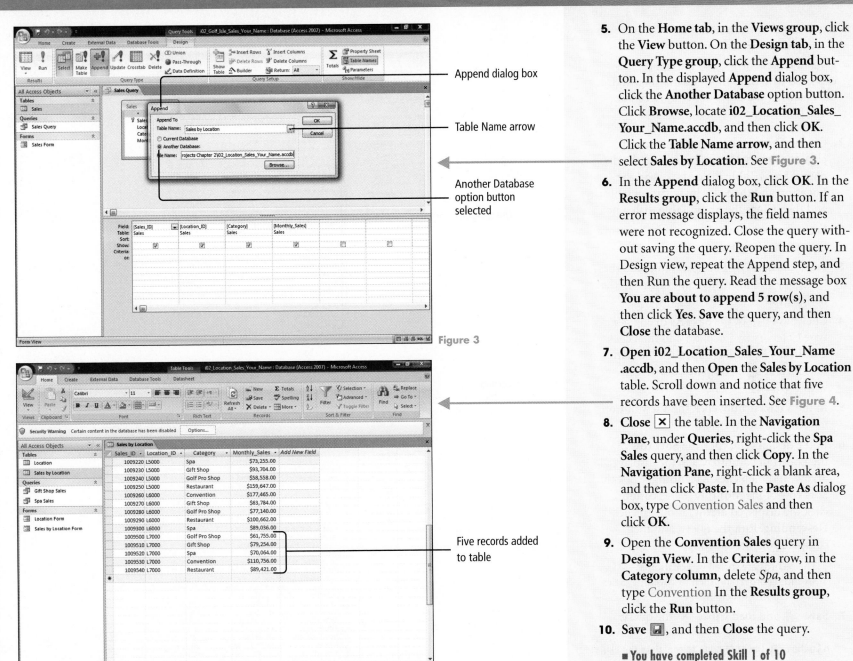

Figure 3

Figure 4

5. On the **Home tab**, in the **Views group**, click the **View** button. On the **Design tab**, in the **Query Type group**, click the **Append** button. In the displayed **Append** dialog box, click the **Another Database** option button. Click **Browse**, locate **i02_Location_Sales_Your_Name.accdb**, and then click **OK**. Click the **Table Name arrow**, and then select **Sales by Location**. See **Figure 3**.

6. In the **Append** dialog box, click **OK**. In the **Results group**, click the **Run** button. If an error message displays, the field names were not recognized. Close the query without saving the query. Reopen the query. In Design view, repeat the Append step, and then Run the query. Read the message box **You are about to append 5 row(s)**, and then click **Yes**. **Save** the query, and then **Close** the database.

7. Open i02_Location_Sales_Your_Name .accdb, and then **Open** the **Sales by Location** table. Scroll down and notice that five records have been inserted. See **Figure 4**.

8. **Close** ✖ the table. In the **Navigation Pane**, under **Queries**, right-click the **Spa Sales** query, and then click **Copy**. In the **Navigation Pane**, right-click a blank area, and then click **Paste**. In the **Paste As** dialog box, type Convention Sales and then click **OK**.

9. Open the **Convention Sales** query in **Design View**. In the **Criteria** row, in the **Category column**, delete *Spa*, and then type Convention In the **Results group**, click the **Run** button.

10. **Save** 🔲, and then **Close** the query.

■ **You have completed Skill 1 of 10**

Append dialog box

Table Name arrow

Another Database option button selected

Five records added to table

▶ Exporting data from Access into Excel creates a copy of the selected data.

▶ Data in tables, forms, and queries can be exported with or without formatting, and the details of the export operation can be saved for future use.

1. On the **Create tab**, in the **Other group**, click the **Query Design** button. In the displayed **Show Table** dialog box, **Add** the **Location** and the **Sales by Location** tables, and then **Close** the **Show Table** dialog box.

2. From the **Location** table, add the **Location** field to the design grid.

3. From the **Sales by Location** table, add the **Category** and **Monthly_Sales** fields to the design grid.

4. Click **Save**. In the **Save As** dialog box, type Category by Location and then click **OK**. In the **Results group**, click the **Run** button, and then compare your screen with **Figure 1**.

5. In the **Views group**, click the **View** button to return to Design view.

6. In the design grid, click the **Sort row** of the **Location column**. Click the displayed **arrow**, and then click **Ascending**. Click the **Sort row** of the **Monthly_Sales column**, click the displayed **arrow**, and then click **Descending**. **Run** the query, and then compare your screen with **Figure 2**.

    The records are sorted by Location in ascending order, and then by Monthly_Sales in descending order.

7. **Save**, and then **Close** the query.

■ **Continue to the next page to complete the skill**

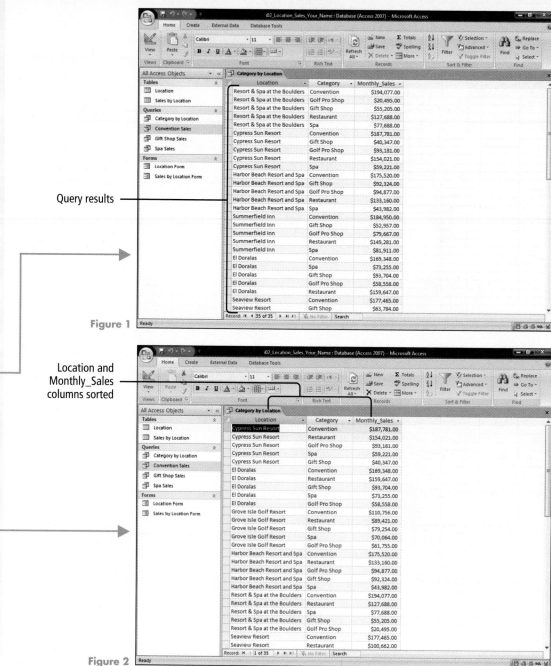

Query results ────

**Figure 1**

Location and Monthly_Sales columns sorted

**Figure 2**

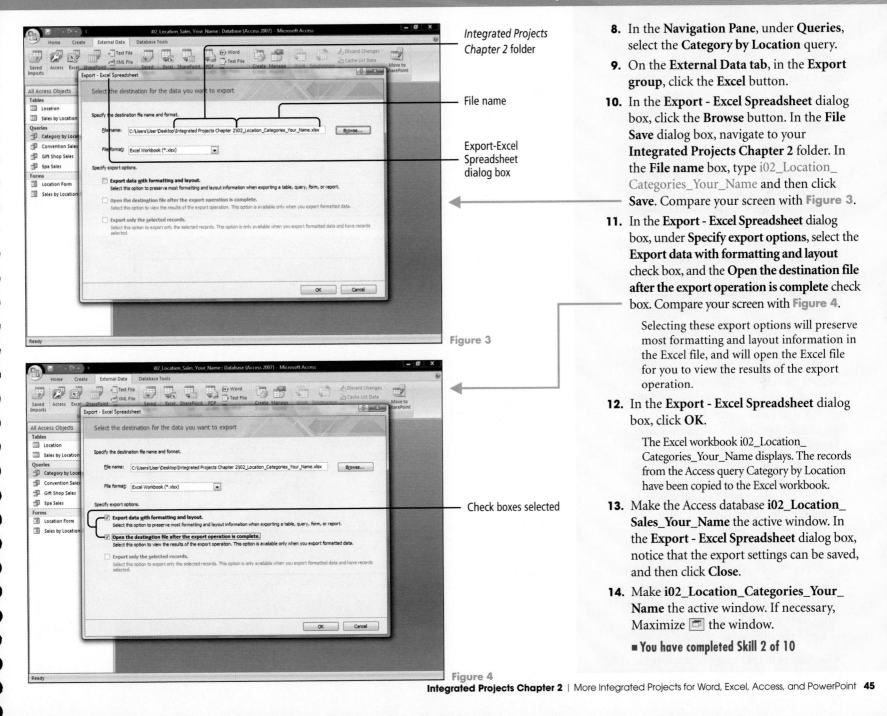

Integrated Projects
Chapter 2 folder

File name

Export-Excel
Spreadsheet
dialog box

Figure 3

Check boxes selected

8. In the **Navigation Pane**, under **Queries**, select the **Category by Location** query.

9. On the **External Data tab**, in the **Export group**, click the **Excel** button.

10. In the **Export - Excel Spreadsheet** dialog box, click the **Browse** button. In the **File Save** dialog box, navigate to your **Integrated Projects Chapter 2** folder. In the **File name** box, type i02_Location_ Categories_Your_Name and then click **Save**. Compare your screen with **Figure 3**.

11. In the **Export - Excel Spreadsheet** dialog box, under **Specify export options**, select the **Export data with formatting and layout** check box, and the **Open the destination file after the export operation is complete** check box. Compare your screen with **Figure 4**.

Selecting these export options will preserve most formatting and layout information in the Excel file, and will open the Excel file for you to view the results of the export operation.

12. In the **Export - Excel Spreadsheet** dialog box, click **OK**.

The Excel workbook i02_Location_ Categories_Your_Name displays. The records from the Access query Category by Location have been copied to the Excel workbook.

13. Make the Access database **i02_Location_ Sales_Your_Name** the active window. In the **Export - Excel Spreadsheet** dialog box, notice that the export settings can be saved, and then click **Close**.

14. Make **i02_Location_Categories_Your_ Name** the active window. If necessary, Maximize the window.

   ■ **You have completed Skill 2 of 10**

▶ A *PivotTable report* is an interactive, cross-tabulated Excel report that summarizes and analyzes data—such as database records—from various sources, including ones that are external to Excel.

▶ In a PivotTable report, each Excel column becomes a PivotTable field that summarizes multiple rows of information.

1. Click cell **A1**. On the **Insert tab**, in the **Tables group**, click the **PivotTable** button. In the displayed **Create PivotTable** dialog box, click **OK**. If the PivotTable Field List pane does not display, on the Options tab, in the Show/Hide group, click the Field List button. In the **PivotTable Field List** pane, select the **Location** check box. See **Figure 1**.

2. In the **PivotTable Field List** pane, drag the **Category** field to the **Report Filter** area. Drag the **Monthly_Sales** field to the **Values** area. In the **Values** area, click the **Sum of Monthly_Sales arrow**, and then click **Value Field Settings**. In the **Value Field Settings** dialog box, in the **Custom Name** box, type Monthly Sales and then click the **Number Format** button. In the **Format Cells** dialog box, click **Currency**, and then change the **Decimal places** to **0**. Click **OK**, and then compare your screen with **Figure 2**.

3. In the **Value Field Settings** dialog box, click **OK**. Select cells **A6:B6**. On the **Home tab**, in the **Font group**, click the **Fill Color button arrow** , and then click **Dark Blue, Text 2, Lighter 60%**—the fourth color in the third row.

   ■ Continue to the next page to complete the skill

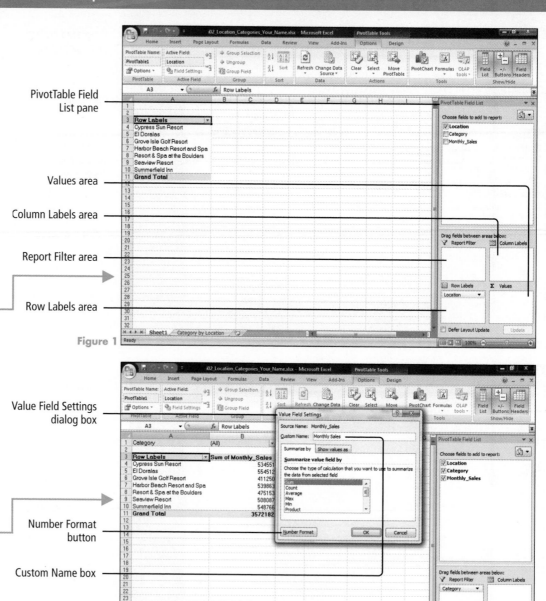

PivotTable Field
List pane

Values area

Column Labels area

Report Filter area

Row Labels area

**Figure 1**

Value Field Settings
dialog box

Number Format
button

Custom Name box

**Figure 2**

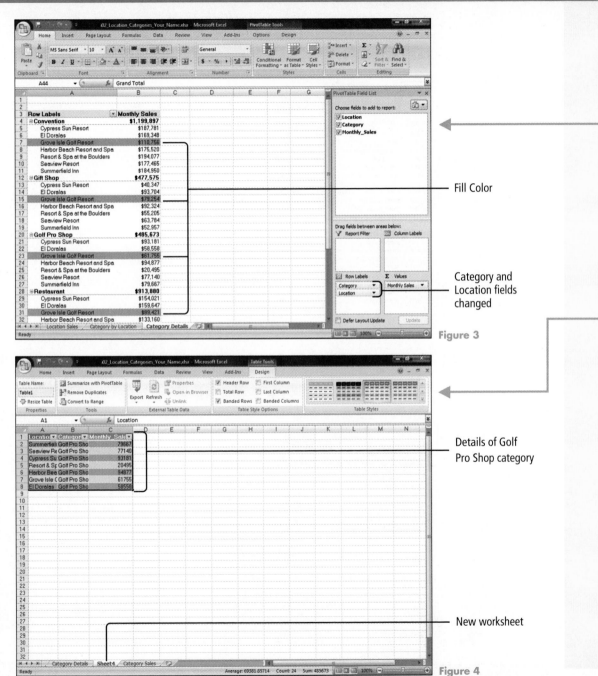

Fill Color

Category and Location fields changed

**Figure 3**

Details of Golf Pro Shop category

New worksheet

**Figure 4**

4. Rename the sheet **Location Sales**, and then **Copy** the worksheet. Rename the new sheet Category Details In the **Report Filter** area, click the **Category arrow**, and then click **Move to Row Labels**. In the **Row Labels** area, drag the **Location** field below the **Category** field. See **Figure 3**.

   The interactive nature of a PivotTable report lets you pivot the fields. Notice the fill color added to row 6 also pivoted and now fills any cell containing Grove Isle Golf Resort.

5. **Copy** the worksheet, and then rename the new sheet Category Sales In the **PivotTable Field List** pane, drag the **Location** field to the **Report Filter** area. Notice the PivotTable report has been pivoted.

6. Double-click cell **B6**—the Monthly Sales for the Golf Pro Shop category. See **Figure 4**.

   A new worksheet containing the Golf Pro Shop category details is created by the *drill-down indicator*—a PivotTable report feature that shows the detailed records of a PivotTable total.

7. Rename the worksheet Golf Pro Shop Select **columns A:C**, and then **AutoFit** the **Column Width**. Select **column C**, and then change the **Cell Style** to **Currency [0]**.

8. Select the first worksheet tab, hold down ⇧ Shift, and then select the last worksheet. **Insert** the file name in the left footer, and then return to **Normal** view. Press Ctrl + Home. Right-click the sheet tab, and then click **Ungroup Sheets**.

9. **Save** 💾 your workbook.

   ■ **You have completed Skill 3 of 10**

▶ Recall that an external reference in Excel is a reference to a cell or range in another Excel workbook.

▶ A *name*—a word or string of characters that represents a cell, range of cells, formula, or constant value—can be used in external references. External references that use names do not change when they are moved or copied.

1. From the **Office menu** 🗐 , click **Open**. Navigate to your student files, and then **Open i02_Inventory.xlsx. Save** 🔲 the workbook in the folder **Integrated Projects Chapter 2** as i02_Inventory_ Your_Name

2. On the **Golf Pro Shop** worksheet, click cell **B2**. See **Figure 1**.

3. Click the **Name Box**, type Golf_Contact and then press Enter. Click cell **C2**. In the **Name Box**, type Golf_Phone and then press Enter.

4. On the **Spa** worksheet, use the same technique to name cell **B2** Spa_Contact and cell **C2** Spa_Phone Click the **Name Box arrow**. See **Figure 2**.

    All names in the workbook are displayed. Names in Excel cannot contain spaces.

5. In the **Name Box**, click **Golf_Contact**. Notice the cell represented by the name—cell **B2** on the **Golf Pro Shop** worksheet—is now the active cell.

6. **Save** 🔲 the workbook. Make **i02_ Location_Categories_Your_Name** the active window. **Insert** a new worksheet, and then rename the worksheet Contacts In cell **A1**, type Inventory Contacts In cell **A3**, type Golf Pro Shop and then in cell **A4**, type Spa

■ **Continue to the next page to complete the skill**

Name box

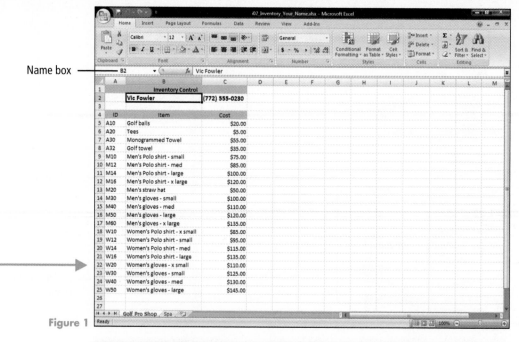

Figure 1

List of Names

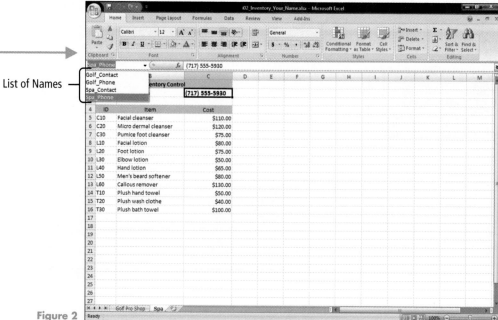

Figure 2

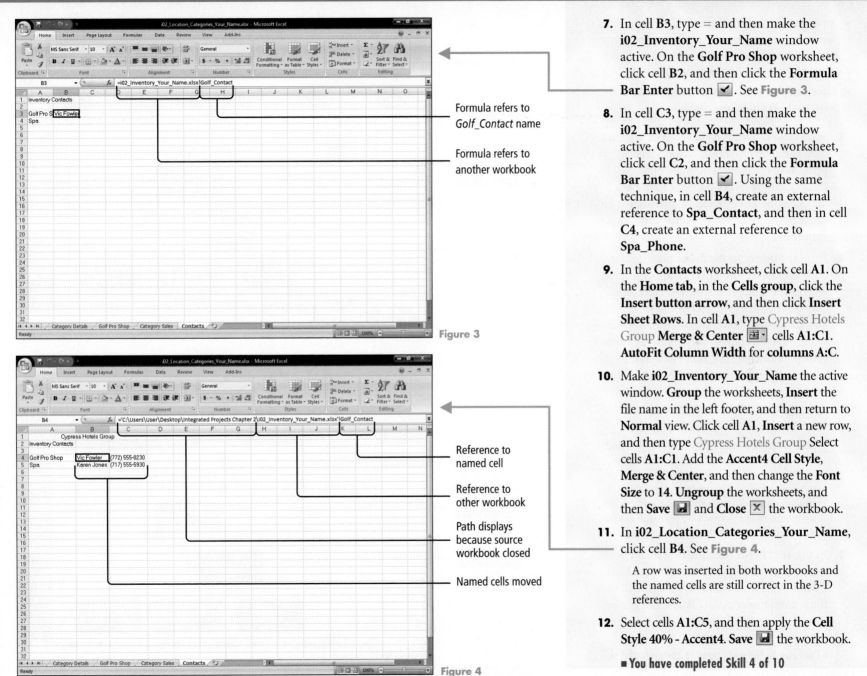

Figure 3

Formula refers to *Golf_Contact* name

Formula refers to another workbook

Reference to named cell

Reference to other workbook

Path displays because source workbook closed

Named cells moved

Figure 4

7. In cell **B3**, type = and then make the **i02_Inventory_Your_Name** window active. On the **Golf Pro Shop** worksheet, click cell **B2**, and then click the **Formula Bar Enter** button ✔. See **Figure 3**.

8. In cell **C3**, type = and then make the **i02_Inventory_Your_Name** window active. On the **Golf Pro Shop** worksheet, click cell **C2**, and then click the **Formula Bar Enter** button ✔. Using the same technique, in cell **B4**, create an external reference to **Spa_Contact**, and then in cell **C4**, create an external reference to **Spa_Phone**.

9. In the **Contacts** worksheet, click cell **A1**. On the **Home tab**, in the **Cells group**, click the **Insert button arrow**, and then click **Insert Sheet Rows**. In cell **A1**, type Cypress Hotels Group **Merge & Center** 🔲 ▾ cells **A1:C1**. **AutoFit Column Width** for **columns A:C**.

10. Make **i02_Inventory_Your_Name** the active window. **Group** the worksheets, **Insert** the file name in the left footer, and then return to **Normal** view. Click cell **A1**, **Insert** a new row, and then type Cypress Hotels Group Select cells **A1:C1**. Add the **Accent4 Cell Style**, **Merge & Center**, and then change the **Font Size** to **14**. **Ungroup** the worksheets, and then **Save** 🔲 and **Close** ✕ the workbook.

11. In **i02_Location_Categories_Your_Name**, click cell **B4**. See **Figure 4**.

    A row was inserted in both workbooks and the named cells are still correct in the 3-D references.

12. Select cells **A1:C5**, and then apply the **Cell Style 40% - Accent4**. **Save** 🔲 the workbook.

■ **You have completed Skill 4 of 10**

► An **organization chart** graphically represents the management structure of an organization, such as department managers and non-management employees within a company.

► Effects and animation can be added to a SmartArt organization chart.

1. **Start** PowerPoint. Navigate to your student files, and then **Open i02_Sales_Meeting. pptx. Save** the presentation in your **Integrated Projects Chapter 2** folder as i02_Sales_Meeting_Your_Name Add the file name in the footer of the **Notes and Handouts.**

2. Display **Slide 6.** In the lower placeholder, click the **Insert SmartArt Graphic** button ⬛. In the **Choose a SmartArt Graphic** dialog box, click **Hierarchy.** Click **Organization Chart,** and then click **OK.** On the **Design tab,** in the **Create Graphic group,** verify that the **Text Pane** button is selected. The **Text pane** is the pane to the left of a SmartArt graphic where the text that appears in the SmartArt graphic can be entered and edited. See **Figure 1.**

   Shapes can be identified by their location and connecting lines. A **superior** is placed above any other shape. An **assistant** is placed below the superior shape, but above subordinates. A **subordinate** is placed below and connected to a superior shape. A **coworker** is next to another shape that is connected to the same superior.

3. In the **Text Pane,** with the first bullet point selected and using your own first and last names, type Your Name and then click in the second bullet point. Type Chet Lee See **Figure 2.**

■ **Continue to the next page to complete the skill**

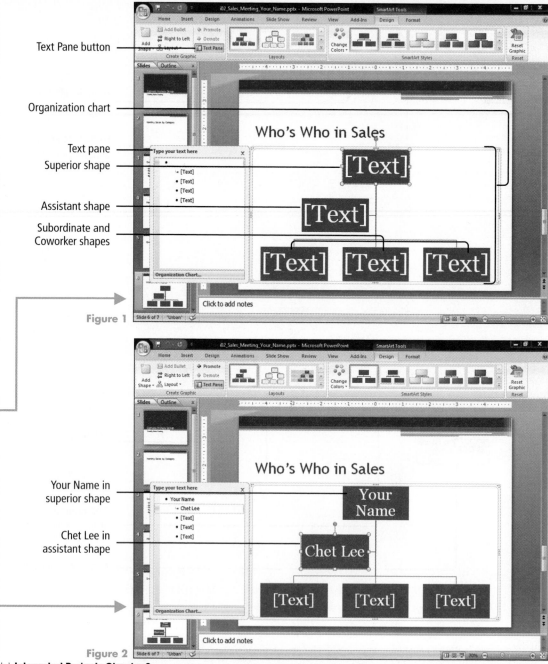

Text Pane button

Organization chart

Text pane
Superior shape

Assistant shape

Subordinate and
Coworker shapes

**Figure 1**

Your Name in
superior shape

Chet Lee in
assistant shape

**Figure 2**

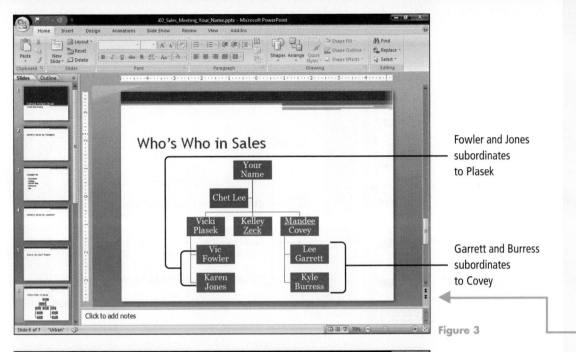

Fowler and Jones subordinates to Plasek

Garrett and Burress subordinates to Covey

Figure 3

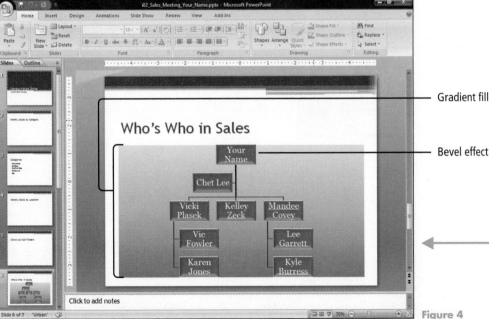

Gradient fill

Bevel effect

Figure 4

4. In the next three bullet points, type Vicki Plasek, Kelley Zeck, and then Mandee Covey In the **Create Graphic group**, click the **Text Pane** button to close the Text pane.

5. Click the first coworker shape—Vicki Plasek. In the **Create Graphic group**, click the **Add Shape button arrow**, and then click **Add Shape Below**. In the new subordinate shape, type Vic Fowler With the Fowler shape selected, click the **Add Shape button arrow**, and then **Add Shape After**. In the new subordinate shape, type Karen Jones

6. Using the same technique, select the shape for **Mandee Covey**, and then add two subordinate shapes with the text Lee Garrett and Kyle Burress Click a blank area of the slide, and then compare your screen with **Figure 3**.

7. Click the organization chart, and then click the border of the placeholder containing the organization chart. On the **Format tab**, in the **Shape Styles group**, click the **Shape Fill** button, and then click **Gray-25%, Background 2**—the third color in the first row. Click the **Shape Fill** button, point to **Gradient**, and then click **Linear Up**—the second variation in the third row.

8. In the **Shape Styles group**, click the **Shape Effects** button. Point to *Bevel*, and then click **Soft Round**—the second effect in the second row under *Bevel*. Click a blank area of the slide, and then compare your screen with **Figure 4**.

9. Save the presentation.

■ **You have completed Skill 5 of 10**

► An Excel PivotTable report can be copied into another Microsoft application.

1. Make **i02_Location_Categories_Your_Name** the active window. If the Category Sales sheet tab is not displayed, at the lower left corner, click the **Tab Scrolling Button to First Worksheet** ⏮. Click the **Next tab** scrolling button ▶ until the **Category Sales sheet tab** is displayed. Click the **Category Sales sheet tab**. Click cell **A5**.

2. On the **Options tab**, in the **Actions group**, click the **Select** button, and then click **Entire PivotTable**. On the **Home tab**, in the **Clipboard group**, click the **Copy** button 🗐.

3. Make **i02_Sales_Meeting_Your_Name.pptx** the active window, and then display **Slide 2**. Click the **Paste button arrow**, and then click **Paste Special**. In the **Paste Special** dialog box, click **Bitmap**, and then click **OK**. On the **Format tab**, in the **Size group**, increase the **Shape Height** ▯ 2″ to **4″**. In the **Arrange group**, click the **Align** button ▭ ▾, and then click **Align Center**. Click a blank section of the slide, and then compare your screen with **Figure 1**.

4. Make **i02_Location_Categories_Your_Name.xlsx** the active window. In cell **B1**, click the arrow. In the displayed filter box, click **Grove Isle Golf Resort**, and then click **OK**. See **Figure 2**.

    The PivotTable report has been filtered to display only the information from the Grove Isle Golf Resort Location.

■ **Continue to the next page to complete the skill** ▶

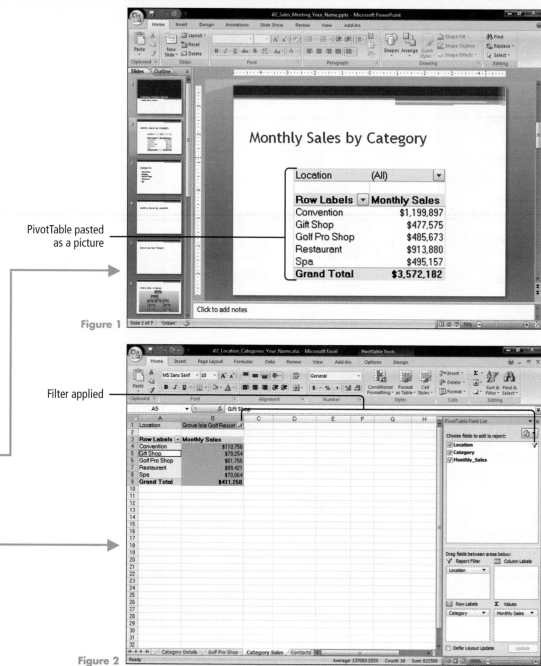

PivotTable pasted as a picture

**Figure 1**

Filter applied

**Figure 2**

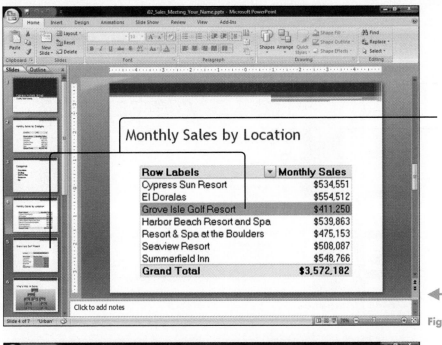

PivotTables pasted into Slides 4 and 5

**Figure 3**

Contact information pasted into Slide 7

**Figure 4**

5. Using the technique from the previous steps, **Select**, and then **Copy** the PivotTable.

6. Make **i02_Sales_Meeting_Your_Name. pptx** the active window.

   The Excel object in Slide 2 did not change because the object was pasted as a picture, not linked to the Excel workbook.

7. Display **Slide 5**. **Paste** the PivotTable as a **Bitmap**, increase the **Shape Height** to 4", and then **Align Center**.

8. Make **i02_Location_Categories_Your_ Name.xlsx** the active window, and then click the **Location Sales sheet tab**. Select, and then **Copy** cells **A3:B11**. Make **i02_Sales_ Meeting_Your_Name.pptx** the active window, and then display **Slide 4**. **Paste** the PivotTable as a **Bitmap**, increase the **Shape Height** to 4", and then **Align Center**. Compare your screen with **Figure 3**.

9. Make **i02_Location_Categories_Your_ Name.xlsx** the active window, and then **Save** the workbook. Click the **Contacts sheet tab**, and then select and **Copy** cells **A1:C5**.

10. Make **i02_Sales_Meeting_Your_Name. pptx** the active window, and then display **Slide 7**. Click the **Paste button arrow**, and then click **Paste Special**. In the **Paste Special** dialog box, click the **Paste link** option button, click **Microsoft Office Excel Worksheet Object**, and then click **OK**. Increase the **Shape Height** to 2.8", **Align Center**, and then compare your screen with **Figure 4**.

11. **Save** the presentation.

   ■ You have completed Skill 6 of 10

► A PowerPoint presentation can be saved as an outline with Outline/RTF. *Rich Text Format (RTF)* is a file format designed to move text between different applications while preserving the text's formatting. This text-only document provides smaller file sizes and the ability to share files with others who may not have the same version of PowerPoint.

► PowerPoint graphics are not included in an Outline/RTF file opened in Word.

1. In **i02_Sales_Meeting_Your_Name.pptx**, click the **Office** button, point to **Save As**, and then click **Other Formats**. In the **Save As** dialog box, navigate to the folder **Integrated Projects Chapter 2**, and then change the file name to i02_Meeting_ Your_Name Click the **Save as type arrow**, and then click **Outline/RTF (*.rtf)**. See **Figure 1**.

2. In the **Save As** dialog box, click **Save**.

3. **Start** Word. From your student files, **Open i02_Meeting_Notes.docx**. **Save** the document in your **Integrated Projects Chapter 2** folder as i02_Meeting_Notes_ Your_Name

4. Scroll down and locate the paragraph beginning *We have been tracking sales*, and then click the first blank line after the paragraph. On the **Insert tab**, in the **Text group**, click the **Object button arrow**, and then click **Text from File**. In the **Insert File** dialog box, navigate to the **Integrated Projects Chapter 2** folder, select **i02_ Meeting_Your_Name.rtf**, and then click **Insert**. See **Figure 2**.

■ **Continue to the next page to complete the skill**

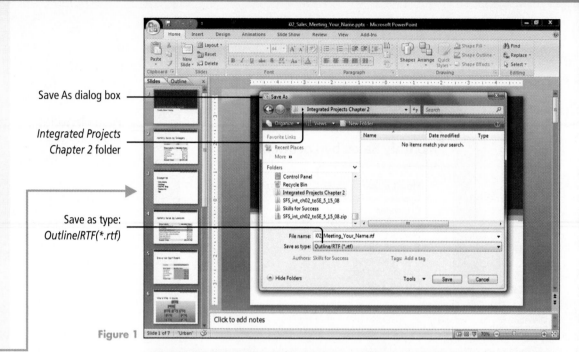

Save As dialog box

*Integrated Projects Chapter 2* folder

Save as type: *Outline/RTF(*.rtf)*

**Figure 1**

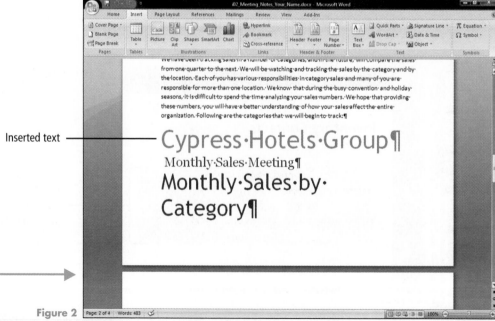

Inserted text

**Figure 2**

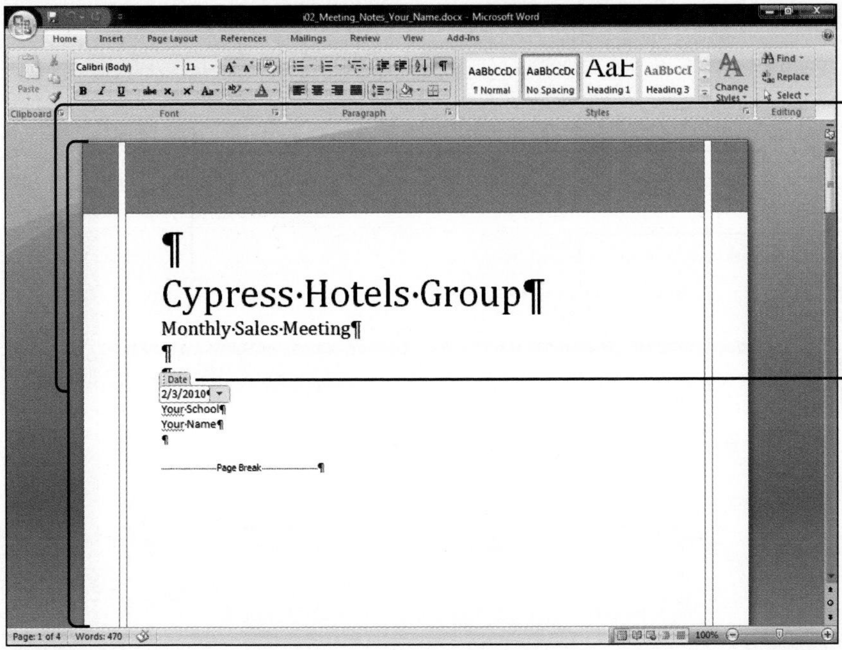


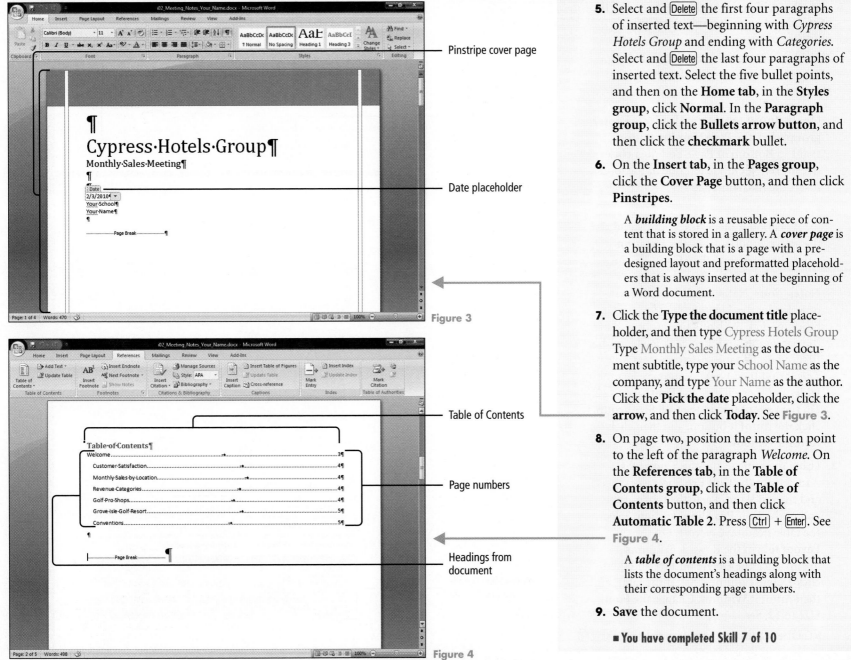

Pinstripe cover page

Date placeholder

Figure 3

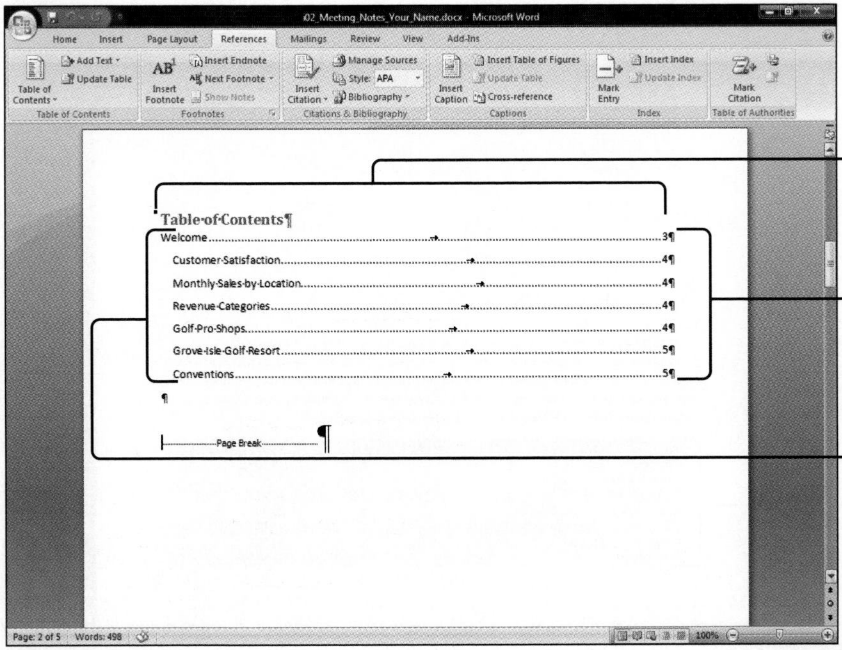


Table of Contents

Page numbers

Headings from document

Figure 4

5. Select and Delete the first four paragraphs of inserted text—beginning with *Cypress Hotels Group* and ending with *Categories.* Select and Delete the last four paragraphs of inserted text. Select the five bullet points, and then on the **Home tab**, in the **Styles group**, click **Normal**. In the **Paragraph group**, click the **Bullets arrow button**, and then click the **checkmark** bullet.

6. On the **Insert tab**, in the **Pages group**, click the **Cover Page** button, and then click **Pinstripes**.

   A ***building block*** is a reusable piece of content that is stored in a gallery. A ***cover page*** is a building block that is a page with a predesigned layout and preformatted placeholders that is always inserted at the beginning of a Word document.

7. Click the **Type the document title** placeholder, and then type Cypress Hotels Group Type Monthly Sales Meeting as the document subtitle, type your School Name as the company, and type Your Name as the author. Click the **Pick the date** placeholder, click the **arrow**, and then click **Today**. See **Figure 3**.

8. On page two, position the insertion point to the left of the paragraph *Welcome*. On the **References tab**, in the **Table of Contents group**, click the **Table of Contents** button, and then click **Automatic Table 2**. Press Ctrl + Enter. See **Figure 4**.

   A ***table of contents*** is a building block that lists the document's headings along with their corresponding page numbers.

9. **Save** the document.

■ **You have completed Skill 7 of 10**

▶ Data that will not change, such as end of the month results, can be embedded into another application.

▶ Data that will change can be linked so data changed in the source file also changes in the destination file.

1. On the **Insert tab**, in the **Header & Footer group**, click the **Page Number** button. Point to **Bottom of Page**, and then click **Accent Bar 4**. On the left side of the footer, insert the file name. See **Figure 1**.

2. **Close** the **Header and Footer**. Make **i02_Location_Categories_Your_Name.xlsx** the active window. Click the **Location Sales sheet tab**, and then **Copy** 📋 the range **A3:B11**. Make **i02_Meeting_Notes_Your_Name.docx** the active window. Under the *Monthly Sales by Location* heading, click the blank line at the end of the paragraph, and then click **Paste**. In the first cell of the table, delete the text *Row Labels*, and then type Locations Select the table, and then change the **Font Size** to **12**. On the **Layout tab**, in the **Cell Size group**, click the **AutoFit** button, and then click **AutoFit Window**.

3. Using the same technique, **Copy** cells **A1:C8** from the **Golf Pro Shop** worksheet, and then in Word, **Paste** the range at the end of the **Golf Pro Shops** section. Select the table heading *Category*. On the **Layout tab**, in the **Rows & Columns group**, click the **Delete** button, and then click **Delete Columns**. Select the table, and then **AutoFit Window**. Change the **Font Size** to **12**. See **Figure 2**.

▪ **Continue to the next page to complete the skill**

Accent Bar 4 page number

File name

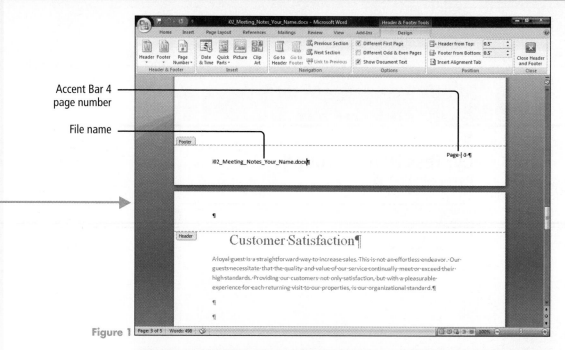

**Figure 1**

Golf Pro Shop Details worksheet data

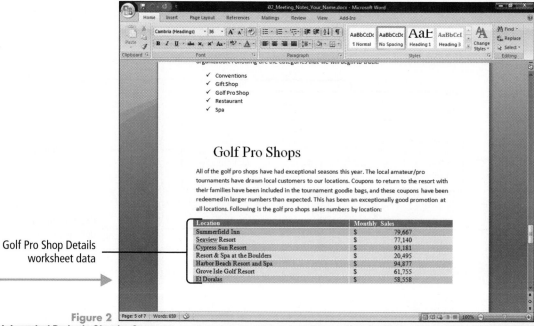

**Figure 2**

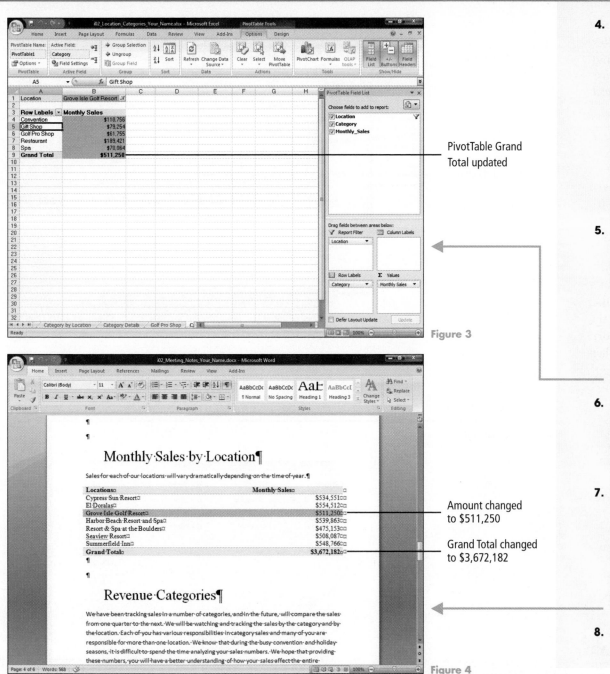

PivotTable Grand
Total updated

Figure 3

Amount changed
to $511,250

Grand Total changed
to $3,672,182

Figure 4

4. Make **i02_Location_Categories_Your_ Name.xlsx** the active window. From the **Category Sales** worksheet, **Copy** cells **A3:B9**. Make **i02_Meeting_Notes_Your_ Name.docx** the active window. Under the *Grove Isle Golf Resort* heading, click the paragraph mark. Click the **Paste button arrow**, and then click **Paste Special**. In the **Paste Special** dialog box, click the **Paste link** option button. Under **As**, click **Microsoft Office Excel Worksheet Object**, and then click **OK**.

5. Right-click the inserted table, point at **Linked Worksheet Object**, and then click **Open Link**. Maximize the workbook. On the **Category by Location** worksheet, change the number in cell **C13** from *$89,421.00* to $189,421.00 Click the **Category Sales** worksheet, and then click cell **A5**. On the **Options tab**, in the **Data group**, click the **Refresh button**. See **Figure 3**.

6. Make **i02_Meeting_Notes_Your_Name.docx** the active window. Notice the Grand Total of the **Grove Isle Golf Resort** PivotTable has been updated. If the total has not changed, right-click the table, and then click **Update Link**.

7. Scroll up to view the table under **Monthly Sales by Location**. Right-click the table, and notice there is no Update Link in the shortcut menu because this is an embedded object, not a linked object. In the **Grove Isle Golf Resort row**, type $511,250 and in the **Grand Total row**, type $3,672,182 See **Figure 4**.

8. **Save** the document.

■ **You have completed Skill 8 of 10**

► An Access table, query, form, or report can be exported from Access to a Word document.

► A *wizard* is a feature that asks questions and then creates an object according to the provided answers. In Access, the *Export Wizard* will export data in a variety of formats, including Excel, Word, and RTF.

1. Make **i02_Location_Sales_Your_Name. accdb** the active window. In the **Navigation Pane**, click the **Conventions Sales** query. On the **External Data tab**, in the **Export group**, click the **Word** button. In the **Export - RTF File** dialog box, click the **Browse** button. Navigate to the **Integrated Projects Chapter 2** folder, change the **File name** to i02_Convention_ Sales_Your_Name and then click **Save**. In the **Export - RTF File** dialog box, select the **Open the destination file after the export operation is complete** check box, and then compare your screen with **Figure 1**.

2. In the **Export - RTF File** dialog box, click **OK**.

   In the Word window, *Compatibility Mode* displays in the title bar to inform the user this is not a Word 2007 document—it is an RTF file.

3. Click the **Office** button, point to **Save As**, and then click **Word Document**. Navigate to the **Integrated Projects Chapter 2** folder, and then **Save** the document as i02_Convention_Sales_Your_ Name Read the displayed message box, click **OK**, and then compare your screen with **Figure 2**.

■ **Continue to the next page to complete the skill**

Export-RTF File dialog box

Selected check box

Compatibility Mode no longer displays

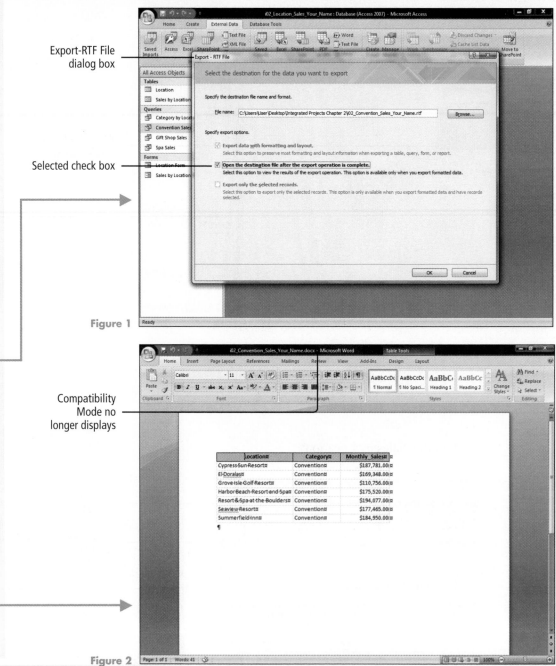

**Figure 1**

**Figure 2**

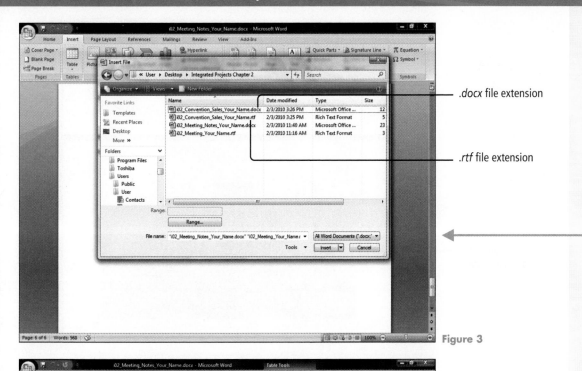

.*docx* file extension

.*rtf* file extension

Figure 3

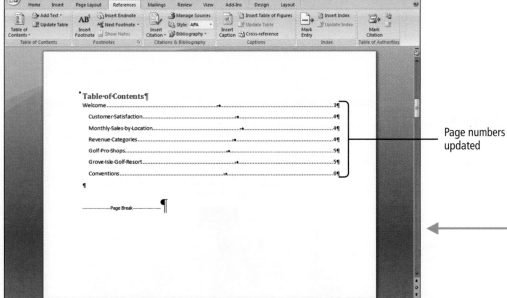

Page numbers
updated

Figure 4

4. **Close** the Word document. In Access, **Close** the **Export - RTF File** dialog box, and then **Exit** Access.

5. Make **i02_Meeting_Notes_Your_Name. docx** the active window. Press [Ctrl] + [End]. On the **Insert tab**, in the **Text group**, click the **Object button arrow**, and then click **Text from File**. In the **Insert File** dialog box, navigate to the **Integrated Projects Chapter 2** folder, and then notice there are two files named **i02_Convention_Sales_ Your_Name**. Compare your screen with **Figure 3**.

   More than one file in a folder can have the same name if the file extensions are different.

6. In the **Insert File** dialog box, click the file **i02_Convention_Sales_Your_Name** ending with the **.docx** file extension, and then click **Insert**. In the first row of the inserted table, click **Category**. On the **Layout tab**, in the **Rows & Columns group**, click the **Delete** button, and then click **Delete Columns**. On the first table row in the second column, replace the underscore character between **Monthly** and **Sales** with a space.

7. Scroll up to display the **Table of Contents**, and then notice the page numbers have not been updated. On the **References tab**, in the **Table of Contents group**, click the **Update Table** button. In the **Update Table of Contents** dialog box, click the **Update entire table** option button, and then click **OK**. Compare your screen with **Figure 4**.

8. **Save** the document.

   ▪ **You have completed Skill 9 of 10**

► Complex objects such as the SmartArt organization chart can be copied from one application to another.

1. Press Ctrl + End, type Our Sales Team and then press Enter. Select the heading **Conventions**, and then on the **Home tab**, in the **Clipboard group**, click the **Format Painter** button. Select the text **Our Sales Team**.

2. Press Ctrl + End, and then type We are fortunate to have a group of people that have quickly melded as a team. Their collaborative effort has resulted in an impressive increase in sales. The structure of our sales team is illustrated in the following organization chart: Press Enter.

3. Make **i02_Sales_Meeting_Your_Name. pptx** the active window, and then display **Slide 6**. Click the border of the placeholder containing the SmartArt organization chart, and then **Copy** the organization chart.

4. Make **i02_Meeting_Notes_Your_Name. docx** the active window. On the **Home tab**, in the **Clipboard group**, click the **Paste** button. Compare your screen with **Figure 1**.

    The SmartArt organization chart, with all the shapes, formatting, and names, is pasted at the end of the document.

5. Place the insertion point to the left of the heading *Our Sales Team*, and then on the **Insert tab**, in the **Pages group**, click the **Page Break** button. Compare your screen with **Figure 2**.

■ **Continue to the next page to complete the skill**

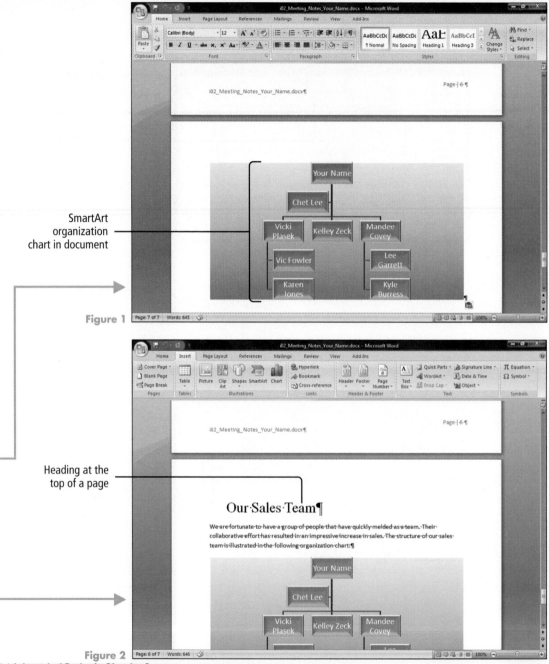

SmartArt organization chart in document

**Figure 1**

Heading at the top of a page

**Figure 2**

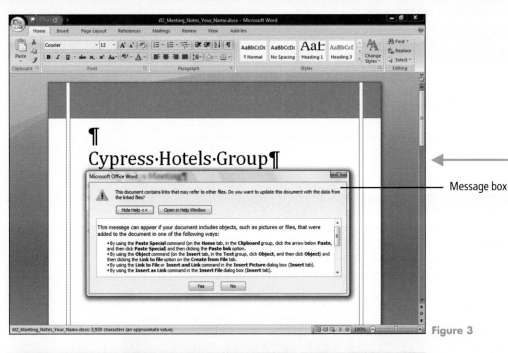

Message box

**Figure 3**

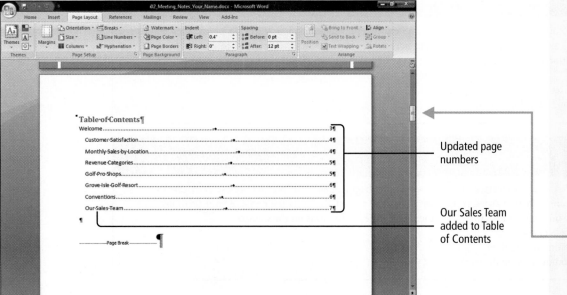

Updated page numbers

Our Sales Team added to Table of Contents

**Figure 4**

6. **Save** the document, and then **Exit** Word. **Save** the presentation, and then **Exit** PowerPoint. **Save** the workbook, and then **Exit** Excel.

7. **Start** 🟢 Word. Navigate to your student files, and then **Open i02_Meeting_Notes_ Your_Name.docx**. In the displayed message box, click **Show Help**, and then compare your screen with **Figure 3**.

   The message box notifies you that there are links in the document and asks if you want to update those links.

8. In the message box, click **Hide Help**, and then click **Yes**. View the Table of Contents and notice the page numbers for *Revenue Categories* and all of the headings that follow it. Press and hold down Ctrl, and then in the **Table of Contents**, click the **Revenue Categories** heading.

   The Table of Contents is linked to each of the document's headings and can be used to navigate to that heading.

9. With the insertion point in front of the **Revenue Categories** heading, **Insert** a **Page Break**. Place the insertion point to the left of the *Grove Isle Golf Resort* heading, and then **Insert** a **Page Break**. View the Table of Contents and notice it does not automatically update. Right-click the **Table of Contents**, and then click **Update Field**. In the **Update Table of Contents** dialog box, click the **Update entire table** option button, and then click **OK**. Click outside of the Table of Contents, and then compare your screen with **Figure 4**.

10. **Save** the document, and then **Exit** Word.

■ **You have completed Skill 10 of 10**

# More Skills

The following More Skills are located at **www.prenhall.com/skills**

## More Skills ⑪ Create an Excel PivotChart and Link the PivotChart to Word

In Excel, a PivotChart report is used to visualize the summary data in a PivotTable report, and to easily see comparisons, patterns, and trends. Both a PivotTable report and a PivotChart report enable you to make informed decisions about critical data in your business.

In More Skills 11, you will create an Excel PivotTable report and a PivotChart report. Then you will open a Word document and link the PivotChart to the document. You will make changes to the source data in Excel and verify that the changes are reflected in the linked PivotChart. To begin, open your Internet browser, navigate to www.prenhall.com/skills, locate the name of your textbook, and then follow the instructions on the website.

## More Skills ⑫ Create a Hyperlink Between PowerPoint, Word, and Excel Files

You can insert a hyperlink for quick access to related information in an existing file, on a Web page, in a specific location of the same file, or to an e-mail address.

In More Skills 12, you will open a Word document and insert hyperlinks to related information in a PowerPoint presentation and in an Excel workbook. To begin, open your Internet browser, navigate to www.prenhall.com/skills, locate the name of your textbook, and then follow the instructions on the website.

## More Skills ⑬ Insert a Total Row in an Excel Table and Link the Table to PowerPoint

In an Excel table, you can display the total row, which displays as the last row in the table. Each cell of the total row contains a drop-down list, so you can select the function that you want to use to calculate the total.

In More Skills 13, you will open an Excel workbook. You will create an Excel table and insert a Total row. You will then link the Excel Table to a PowerPoint Presentation. To begin, open your Internet browser, navigate to www.prenhall.com/skills, locate the name of your textbook, and then follow the instructions on the website.

## More Skills ⑭ Compare Word Documents

If you send a document for review to several reviewers, and each reviewer returns the document containing their changes, you can combine the documents two at a time until all the reviewer changes have been incorporated into a single document.

In More Skills 14, you will open a document and then compare it with documents containing comments from different reviewers. To begin, open your Internet browser, navigate to www.prenhall.com/skills, locate the name of your textbook, and then follow the instructions on the website.

# Key Terms

# Online Help Skills

1.  **Start** your Web browser, for example Internet Explorer. In the **Address Bar**, type www.microsoft.com/powerpoint and then press [Enter] to display the **PowerPoint Home Page** for Microsoft Office Online.

2.  In the upper left portion of the screen, click the text **Search PowerPoint 2007** in the search box, type fluent interface and then press [Enter]. In the list of results, click **Demo: The new PowerPoint 2007 Fluent interface**. Take a moment to read the information. Then, turn on your speakers or put on headphones, scroll down if necessary, and click **Play Demo**. The demo will begin as shown in **Figure 1**, and is only a few minutes in length.

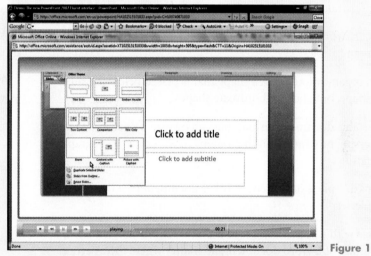

Figure 1

3.  Listen to and watch the demonstration, and then see if you can answer the following question: How does the Slide Library help make consistent presentations?

# Matching

Match each term in the second column with its correct definition in the first column by writing the letter of the term on the blank line in front of the correct definition.

_____ **1.** An interactive, cross-tabulated Excel report that summarizes and analyzes data.

_____ **2.** A PivotTable report feature that shows the detailed records of a PivotTable total.

_____ **3.** A word or string of characters that represents a cell, range of cells, formula, or constant value.

_____ **4.** A SmartArt object that represents the management structure of an organization.

_____ **5.** In an organization chart, a shape that is placed below the superior shape, but above subordinate shapes.

_____ **6.** A portable document format that can be read by nearly all word-processing programs and that retains most text and paragraph formatting.

_____ **7.** A reusable piece of content or other document part that is stored in galleries.

_____ **8.** A page with a predesigned layout that is always inserted at the beginning of a Word document, no matter where the insertion point appears in the document.

_____ **9.** A feature that asks questions and then creates an item according to the provided answers.

_____ **10.** In Access, a feature that will export data in a variety of formats.

**A** Assistant

**B** Building block

**C** Cover page

**D** Drill-down indicator

**E** Export Wizard

**F** Name

**G** Organization chart

**H** PivotTable report

**I** Rich Text Format

**J** Wizard

# Fill in the Blank

Write the correct answer in the space provided.

1. An Access _____ query is a query that adds a set of records from one or more source tables to one or more destination tables.

2. When exporting data from Access to Excel, selecting the _____ option check boxes will preserve most formatting and layout information.

3. In a PivotTable report, each Excel column becomes a PivotTable _____ that summarizes multiple rows of information.

4. A _____ reference in Excel is a reference to a cell or range in another Excel workbook.

5. The pane to the left of a SmartArt graphic where the text that appears in the SmartArt graphic can be entered and edited is called a _____ pane.

6. In an organization chart, a _____ shape is a shape that is placed above any other shape.

7. In an organization chart, a _____ shape is a shape that is placed below and connected to a superior shape.

8. In an organization chart, a _____ shape is next to another shape that is connected to the same superior shape.

9. A cover page or a table of contents is an example of a _____ block.

10. A list of the headings in a document that will provide an overview of the topics discussed is called a _____ of contents.

# Topics for Discussion

1. Integration lets you move data between the Microsoft applications. How does integration help when analyzing data?

2. How can integration help a team present their ideas and results to management?

# Skill Check 1

**To complete these files, you will need the following files:**

- i02_Golf_Presentation.pptx
- i02_Golf_Report.docx

**You will save your files as:**

- i02_Golf_Outline_Your_Name.rtf
- i02_Golf_Presentation_Your_Name.pptx
- i02_Golf_Report_Your_Name.docx

1. **Start** PowerPoint. Navigate to your student files, and then **Open i02_Golf_Presentation**. **Save** the presentation in the **Integrated Projects Chapter 2** folder as i02_Golf_Presentation_Your_Name Add the file name in the footer of the **Notes and Handouts**.

2. Display **Slide 5**. In the placeholder, click the **Insert SmartArt Graphic** button. In the **Choose a SmartArt Graphic** dialog box, click **List**. In the **Choose a SmartArt Graphic** dialog box, click **Basic Block List**—the first subtype—and then click **OK**. If necessary, on the Design tab, in the Create Graphic group, click the Text Pane button to display the Text pane.

3. In the **Text pane**, type the following locations: Cypress Sun Resort, Grove Isle Golf Resort, Resort & Spa at the Boulders, Harbor Beach Resort and Spa, and El Doralas Press [Enter], type Seaview Resort and then compare your screen with **Figure 1**.

4. In the **Create Graphic group**, click the **Text Pane** button. In the **SmartArt Styles group**, click the **More** button. Click **Cartoon**—the third style in the first row under *3-D*. Click the **Change Colors** button, and then under **Accent 2**, click **Transparent Gradient Range - Accent 2**—the last color in the row. Compare your screen with **Figure 2**.

5. On the **View tab**, in the **Presentation Views group**, click the **Slide Show** button, and then view the presentation. **Save** the presentation.

6. Click the **Office** button, point to **Save As**, and then click **Other Formats**. In the **Save As** dialog box, navigate to the folder **Integrated Projects Chapter 2**, and then change the file name to i02_Golf_Outline_Your_Name Click the **Save as type arrow**, and then click **Outline/RTF (*.rtf)**. Click **Save**.

■ Continue to the next page to complete Skill Check 1

Figure 1

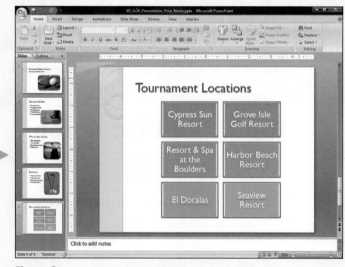

Figure 2

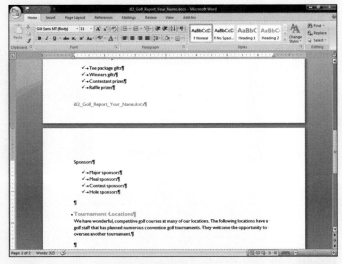

**Figure 3**

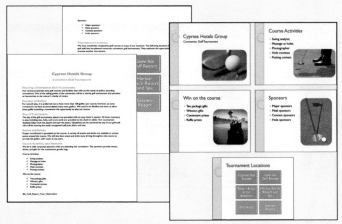

**Figure 4**

7. **Start** Word. Navigate to your student files, and then **Open i02_Golf_Report**. **Save** the document in the **Integrated Projects Chapter 2** folder as i02_Golf_Report_ Your_Name and then **Insert** the file name into the footer.

8. Move the insertion point to the end of the document. On the **Insert tab**, in the **Text group**, click the **Object button arrow**, and then click **Text from File**. In the **Insert File** dialog box, navigate to the **Integrated Projects Chapter 2** folder, select the RTF file **i02_Golf_Outline_Your_Name**, and then click **Insert**.

9. Select the first two paragraphs of inserted text—*Cypress Hotels Group* and *Convention Golf Tournament*— and then Delete the paragraphs. Select the remaining inserted text. On the **Home tab**, in the **Styles group**, click the **Normal** style.

10. Select the five paragraphs beginning with *Swing analysis*, and then on the **Home tab**, in the **Paragraph group**, click the **Bullets button arrow**, and then click the **check mark** bullet. Select the four paragraphs beginning with *Tee package gifts*, and then add the **check mark** bullets. Select the four paragraphs beginning with *Major sponsors*, and then add the **check mark** bullets.

11. Select the heading *Course Activities and Sponsors*, and then on the **Home tab**, in the **Clipboard group**, click the **Format Painter** button. At the end of the document, select the text *Tournament Locations*. Place the insertion point after the *Tournament Locations* heading, and then type We have wonderful, competitive golf courses at many of our locations. The following locations have a golf staff that has planned numerous convention golf tournaments. They welcome the opportunity to oversee another tournament. Press Enter, and then compare your screen with **Figure 3**.

12. Make **i02_Golf_Presentation_Your_Name** the active window, and then display **Slide 5**. Click the border of the placeholder containing the SmartArt, and then **Copy** the SmartArt.

13. Make **i02_Golf_Report_Your_Name** the active window. Move the insertion point to the end of the document, and then on the **Home tab**, in the **Clipboard group**, click the **Paste** button.

14. Compare your screen with the completed documents in **Figure 4**. **Save**, and then **Close** the files. Submit your files as directed.

**Done!** You have completed Skill Check 1

# Skill Check 2

## To complete these files, you will need the following files:

- New blank Excel workbook
- i02_Employees.accdb
- i02_Housekeeping.accdb
- i02_Restaurant.accdb

## You will save your files as:

- i02_All_Employees_Your_Name.accdb
- i02_Housekeeping_Your_Name.accdb
- i02_Restaurant_Your_Name.accdb
- i02_Employees_Your_Name.xlsx

1. **Start** Access. From your student data files, **Open i02_Employees**. Click the **Office** button, point to **Save As**, and then click **Access 2007 Database**. Navigate to the **Integrated Projects Chapter 2** folder. **Save** the database as i02_All_Employees_ Your_Name and then **Close** the database.

2. From your student data files, **Open i02_Housekeeping**, and then **Save** the database in the **Integrated Projects Chapter 2** folder as i02_Housekeeping_Your_ Name If the Security Warning message displays, enable the content. On the **Create tab**, in the **Other group**, click the **Query Wizard** button. In the **New Query** dialog box, click **Simple Query Wizard**, and then click **OK**. Click the **Move All** button, and then compare your screen with **Figure 1**.

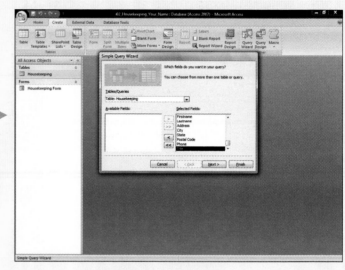

**Figure 1**

3. In the **Simple Query Wizard** dialog box, click **Finish**. On the **Home tab**, in the **Views group**, click the **View** button. On the **Design tab**, in the **Query Type** group, click the **Append** button. In the **Append** dialog box, click the **Another Database** option button. Click **Browse**, locate i02_All_Employees_Your_Name, and then click **OK**. Click the **Table Name** arrow, and then select **Employees**. Compare your screen with **Figure 2**.

4. In the **Append** dialog box, click **OK**. In the **Results group**, click the **Run** button. In the message box **You are about to append 41 row(s)**, click **Yes**. If an error message displays, close the query without saving the query. Reopen the query. In Design view, repeat the Append step, and then Run the query. **Save** the query, and then **Close** the database.

5. **Open i02_Restaurant**, and then **Save** the database in the **Integrated Projects chapter 2** folder as i02_Restaurant_Your_Name. If necessary, enable the content.

■ Continue to the next page to complete Skill Check 2

**Figure 2**

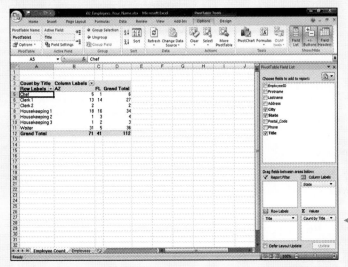

**Figure 3**

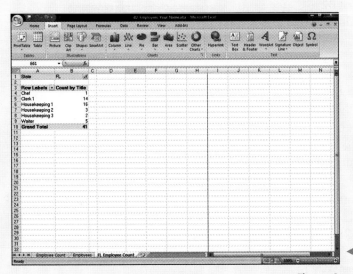

**Figure 4**

6. On the **Create tab**, in the **Other group**, click the **Query Wizard** button. In the **New Query** dialog box, click **Simple Query Wizard**, and then click **OK**. Click the **Move All** button, and then click **Finish**. On the **Home tab**, in the **Views group**, click the **View** button. On the **Design tab**, in the **Query Type** group, click the **Append** button. In the **Append** dialog box, click the **Another Database** option button. Click **Browse**, locate **i02_All_Employees_Your_Name**, and then click **OK**. Click the **Table Name arrow**, and then select **Employees**. In the **Append** dialog box, click **OK**. In the **Results group**, click the **Run** button. If an error message displays, close the query without saving the query. Reopen the query. In Design view, repeat the Append step, and then Run the query. In the message box **You are about to append 42 row(s)**, click **Yes**. **Save** the query, and then **Close** the database.

7. **Open i02_All_Employees_Your_Name**. In the **Navigation Pane**, click the **Employees** table. On the **External Data tab**, in the **Export group**, click the **Excel** button. In the **Export - Excel Spreadsheet** dialog box, click the **Browse** button. In the **File Save** dialog box, navigate to your **Integrated Projects Chapter 2** folder. Type the file name i02_Employees_Your_Name and then click **Save**. Under **Specify export options**, select the **Export data with formatting and layout** check box, and then click **OK**. **Close** the dialog box, and then **Exit** Access.

8. **Start** Excel, and then open **i02_Employees_Your_Name**. Click cell **A1**. On the **Insert tab**, in the **Tables group**, click the **PivotTable** button. In the **Create PivotTable** dialog box, click **OK**. If necessary, display the PivotTable Field List pane.

9. In the **PivotTable Field List** pane, drag the **Title** field to the **Row Labels** area, and then drag the **State** field to the **Columns Labels** area. Drag the **City** field to the **Values** area. In the **Values** area, click the **Count of City arrow**, and then click **Value Field Settings**. In the **Value Field Settings** dialog box, in the **Custom Name** box, type Count by Title under **Summarize value field by**, click **Count**, and then click **OK**. Rename the sheet Employee Count, and then compare your screen with **Figure 3**.

10. Create a copy of the **Employee Count** worksheet, and then rename the new sheet as FL Employee Count In the **PivotTable Field List** pane, drag the **State** field from the **Column Labels** area to the **Report Filter** area. In cell **B1**, click the arrow. From the displayed list, click **FL**, and then click **OK**.

11. **Group** the worksheets, **Insert** the file name in the left footer, and then return to **Normal** view. **Ungroup** the worksheets.

12. Compare your screen with the completed document in **Figure 4**. **Save,** and then **Close** the files. Submit your files as directed.

**Done!** You have completed Skill Check 2

# Assess Your Skills 1

## To complete these files, you will need the following files:

- i02_Phoenix_Memo.docx
- i02_Golf.xlsx
- i02_Spa.xlsx
- i02_Gifts.xlsx
- i02_Phoenix_Inventory.xlsx

## You will save your files as:

- i02_Phoenix_Memo_Your_Name.docx
- i02_Phoenix_Inventory_Your_Name.xlsx

1. **Start** Excel, and then **Open i02_Phoenix_Inventory**. **Save** the file in your **Integrated Projects Chapter 2** folder as i02_Phoenix_Inventory_Your_Name and then insert the file name in the left footer. Return to **Normal** view.

2. **Open** the Excel files **i02_Gifts**, **i02_Golf**, and **i02_Spa**. Make **i02_Phoenix_Inventory_Your_Name** the active window. In cell **B4**, create a 3-D reference to cell **D17** in the workbook **i02_Gifts**, and then in cell **C4**, create a 3-D reference to cell **E17** in **i02_Gifts**.

3. In cell **B5**, create a 3-D reference to cell **D34** in the workbook **i02_Golf**, and then in cell **C5**, create a 3-D reference to cell **E34** in **i02_Golf**. In cell **B6**, create a 3-D reference to cell **D14** in the workbook **i02_Spa**, and then in cell **C6**, create a 3-D reference to cell **E14** in **i02_Spa**.

4. In cells **B7:C7**, use the SUM function to total **columns B and C**. Format cells **C4:C7** with the Currency Number style. Select cells **B7:C7** and apply a **Top Border**. **Save** the workbook. Close the Excel files **i02_Gifts**, **i02_Golf**, and **i02_Spa**.

5. **Start** Word, and then **Open i02_Phoenix_Memo**. **Save** the document in your **Integrated Projects Chapter 2** folder as i02_Phoenix_Memo_Your_Name and then insert the file name in the footer.

6. Make **i02_Phoenix_Inventory_Your_Name** the active window. Select the range **A1:C7**, and then **Copy** the range. Make **i02_Phoenix_Memo_Your_Name** the active window. Move the insertion point to the end of the document, and then use **Paste Special** to link the Excel data to the Word document as a **Microsoft Office Excel Worksheet Object**.

7. Right-click the inserted table, point to **Linked Worksheet Object**, and then click **Open Link**. **Maximize** the workbook. Change cell **B2** to Phoenix Inventory - June 15, 2010 change cell **A4** to Gift Shop and then change cell **A5** to Golf Pro Shop

8. **Save** the Excel workbook. Make **i02_Phoenix_Memo_Your_Name** the active window. Right-click the table, and then click **Update Link**.

9. At the top of the document, after the heading **FROM**, replace *Your Name* with your first and last names.

10. Compare your completed documents with **Figure 1**. **Save** your document, and then **Exit** Word. **Exit** Excel. Submit your files as directed by your instructor.

**Done!** You have completed Assess Your Skills 1

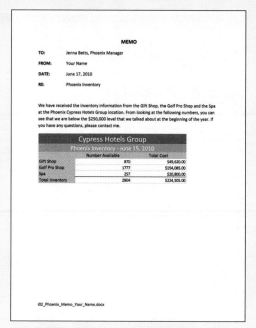

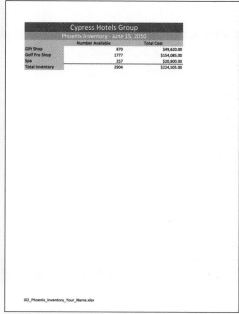

Figure 1

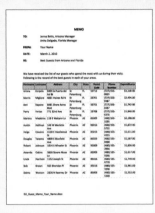

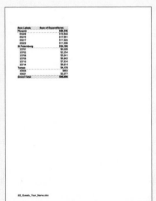

Figure 1

# Assess Your Skills 2

## To complete these files, you will need the following files:

- New blank Excel workbook
- i02_Guests.accdb
- i02_Guest_Memo.docx

## You will save your files as:

- i02_Guests_Your_Name.xlsx
- i02_Guest_Memo_Your_Name.docx
- i02_Best_Guests_Your_Name.rtf

1. **Start** Access, and then **Open i02_Guests**. In the **Navigation Pane**, click the **Guests** table. Export the table to an Excel workbook. **Save** the file in your **Integrated Projects Chapter 2** folder as i02_Guests_Your_Name Export the data with the formatting and layout.

2. **Run Best Guests** query. Notice the query lists the guests with expenditures over $1,500. Export the query results as a RTF file. **Save** the RTF file in your **Integrated Projects Chapter 2** folder as i02_Best_Guests_Your_Name **Close** the database, and then **Exit** Access.

3. **Start** Excel, and then **Open i02_Guests_Your_Name**. For the data in cells **A1:H95**, insert a PivotTable on a new sheet. In the **PivotTable Field List** pane, drag the **City** field and then the **Postal Code** field to the **Row Labels** area. Drag the **Expenditures** field to the **Values** area. **Open** the **Value Field Settings** dialog box, and then change the **Number Format** to **Currency** with zero decimal places. Rename the worksheet Expenditures by Postal Code and then **Insert** the file name in the left footer of both worksheets. **Save** the workbook.

4. **Start** Word, and then **Open i02_Guest_Memo**. **Save** the file in your **Integrated**

Projects Chapter 2 folder as i02_Guest_Memo_Your_Name and then add the file name to the footer. At the top of the document, after **FROM**, replace *Your Name* with your first and last names.

5. Move the insertion point to the end of the document. Insert the RTF file **i02_Best_Guests_Your_Name**, and then resize the table cells to **AutoFit Window**.

6. Move to the end of the document, and then type We have provided the sales information organized by Postal Code so you can see the result of the new promotional materials. If you have any questions, please contact me. Press Enter.

7. Make **i02_Guests_Your_Name** the active window, and then on the **Expenditures by Postal Code** worksheet, **Copy** the range **A4:B19**. Make **i02_Guest_Memo_Your_Name** the active window. At the end of the document, **Paste** the Excel data. Select the table, and then change the **Font Size** to **12**.

8. Compare your completed documents with **Figure 1**. **Save** your files, and then **Exit** Word and **Exit** Excel. Submit your files as directed by your instructor.

**Done!** You have completed Assess Your Skills 2

# Assess Your Skills 3

**To complete these files, you will need the following files:**

- i02_Convention_Memo.docx
- i02_Convention_Presentation.pptx

**You will save your files as:**

- i02_Convention_List_Your_Name.rtf
- i02_Convention_Memo_Your_Name.docx

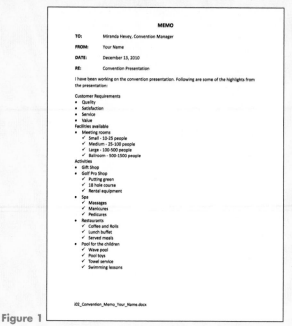

**Figure 1**

1. **Start** PowerPoint, and then **Open i02_Convention_Presentation**. Display **Slide 4**. Under **Restaurants**, add three bullet points: Coffee and Rolls, Lunch buffet, and Served meals These three bullet points should be indented and look the same as the bullet points under *Golf Pro Shop*.

2. **Save** the presentation as an Outline/RTF file in your **Integrated Projects Chapter 2** folder as i02_Convention_List_Your_Name **Close** the presentation. When asked, do not save the presentation. **Exit** PowerPoint.

3. **Start** Word, and then **Open i02_Convention_Memo**. **Save** the document in your **Integrated Projects Chapter 2** folder as i02_Convention_Memo_Your_Name and then insert the file name in the footer. At the top of the document, after **FROM**, replace *Your Name* with your first and last names.

4. Place the insertion point at the end of the document. **Insert** the text from the RTF file i02_Convention_List_Your_Name.

5. Select the inserted text. Change the **Font** to **Calibri**, the **Font Size** to **12**, and the **Font Color** to **Automatic**.

6. Delete the first two paragraphs of inserted text, *Cypress Hotels Group* and *Conventions*.

7. Select the ten paragraphs with the bull's-eye bullet—starting with *Quality* and ending with *Pool for the children*. On the **Home tab**, click the **Bullets button arrow**, and then click the solid round bullet. Select all other bullet points, excluding the paragraphs *Customer Requirements*, *Facilities available*, and *Activities*. Click the **Bullets button arrow**, and then click the **check mark**. Select the first four paragraphs with the check mark bullet points, and then click the **Increase Indent** button.

8. Verify that the document is a one-page document. If not, move the insertion point to the end of the document and delete any blank lines.

9. Compare your completed document with **Figure 1**. **Save** your file, and then submit your file as directed by your instructor.

   **Done!** You have completed Assess Your Skills 3

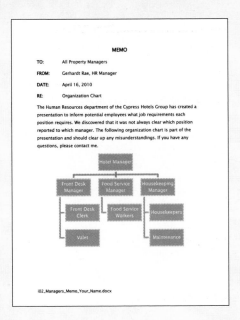

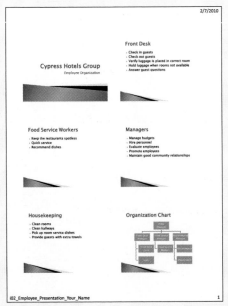

Figure 1

# Assess Your Skills 4

## To complete these files, you will need the following files:

- i02_Employee_Presentation.pptx
- i02_Managers_Memo.docx

## You will save your files as:

- i02_Employee_Presentation_Your_Name.pptx
- i02_Managers_Memo_Your_Name.docx

1. **Start** PowerPoint, and then **Open i02_Employee_Presentation**. **Save** the presentation in your **Integrated Projects Chapter 2** folder as i02_Employee_Presentation_Your_Name and then type the file name in the **Notes and Handouts footer**.

2. Display **Slide 6**, and then in the lower placeholder, click the **Insert SmartArt Graphic** button. Click **Hierarchy**, and then click **Organization Chart**. In the superior shape, type Hotel Manager and then delete the assistant shape. In the three subordinate shapes, type Front Desk Manager, Food Service Manager, and Housekeeping Manager

3. Under the shape **Front Desk Manager**, add two subordinate shapes, and then in the shapes type Front Desk Clerk and Valet

4. Under the shape **Food Service Manager**, add a subordinate shape, and then in the shape type Food Service Workers

5. Under the shape **Housekeeping Manager**, add two subordinate shapes, and then in the shapes type Housekeepers and Maintenance **Save** the presentation.

6. **Start** Word, and then **Open i02_Managers_Memo**. **Save** the document in your **Integrated Projects Chapter 2** folder as i02_Managers_Memo_Your_Name and then **Insert** the file name in the footer. Place the insertion point at the end of the paragraph beginning *The Human Resources department*, and then type The following organization chart is part of the presentation and should clear up any misunderstandings. If you have any questions, please contact me.

7. Make **i02_Employee_Presentation_Your_Name** the active window. On **Slide 6**, click the placeholder border to select the SmartArt organization chart, and then **Copy** the chart.

8. Make **i02_Managers_Memo_Your_Name** the active window, and then place the insertion point at the end of the document. **Paste** the organization chart. If necessary, resize the organization chart so it displays at the bottom of the first page.

9. Compare your completed documents with **Figure 1**. **Save** your files, and then **Exit** Word and **Exit** PowerPoint. Submit your files as directed by your instructor.

**Done! You have completed Assess Your Skills 4**

# Glossary

**3-D reference** A reference for the same cell or range on multiple worksheets that follow the same pattern.

**Adjustment handle** A diamond-shaped handle used to adjust the appearance but not the size of most objects.

**Append query** An Access query that adds records to a destination table.

**Assistant** In an organization chart, a shape that is placed below the superior shape, but above subordinate shapes.

**AutoExpansion** An Excel feature that automatically includes an adjoining column into an Excel table.

**Building block** A reusable piece of content or other document part that is stored in a gallery.

**Calculated column** An Excel table feature that uses a single formula that adjusts for each row, and automatically expands to include additional rows so that the formula is immediately extended to those rows.

**Cover page** A page with a predesigned layout that is always inserted at the beginning of a Word document and contains preformatted placeholders.

**Coworker** In an organization chart, a shape next to another shape that is connected to the same superior shape.

**Criteria** Conditions you specify to limit choices.

**Data source** The part of the Word mail merge feature that contains the information, such as names and addresses, that changes with each letter or label.

**Destination file** A file that a linked or embedded object is inserted into.

**Drill-down indicator** A PivotTable report feature that shows the detailed records of a PivotTable total.

**Embedded object** An object that becomes part of the destination file. If the source file is modified the embedded object does not change.

**Excel table** A series of rows and columns that contains related data that is managed independently from the data in other rows and columns on the worksheet.

**Export Wizard** In Access, a feature that will export data in a variety of formats, including Excel, Word, and RTF.

**External reference** Creates a reference between objects in different files.

**File extension** A set of characters added to the end of a file name that identifies the file type.

**Filter** A feature that hides Excel rows or Access records that do not meet certain criteria.

**Filter drop-down list** A control that displays a list of filter and sort options for a column in an Excel table or Access datasheet.

**Linked Object** An object that maintains a connection between the source and destination files. Linked data or objects are stored in the source file. If the source file is modified the linked object is also modified.

**Main document** The part of the Word mail merge feature that contains the text that remains constant.

**Name** A word or string of characters that represents a cell, range of cells, formula, or constant value.

**Object linking and embedding** A program-integration technology that shares information between programs through linked or embedded objects.

**OLE** See object linking and embedding.

**Organization chart** Graphically represents the management structure of an organization, such as department managers and non-management employees within a company.

**PivotChart report** A graphical representation of the data in a PivotTable report.

**PivotTable report** An interactive, crosstabulated Excel report that summarizes and analyzes data—such as database records—from various sources, including ones that are external to Excel.

**Rich Text Format** A universal document format that can be read by nearly all word-processing programs and that retains most text and paragraph formatting.

**RTF** See Rich Text Format.

**Shape** An object that can be inserted to emphasize a point. A shape can be any one of a variety of objects such as stars, banners, and callouts.

**Shape effect** A predesigned format that makes the shape look more professional.

**Shared workbook** An Excel workbook that allows different users to view and make changes in the workbook at the same time.

**Shortcut menu** A menu that shows a list of commands relevant to a particular item and is displayed when you right-click an item.

**Source file** A file that contains the original information that is used to create a linked or embedded object.

**Subordinate** In an organization chart, a shape that is placed below and connected to a superior shape.

**Superior** In an organization chart, a shape that is placed above any other shape.

**Synchronous scrolling** Both Word documents scroll together.

**Table of contents** A list of the headings in a document that will provide an overview of the topics discussed in a document.

**Text box** A movable, resizable container for text or graphics.

**Text pane** The pane to the left of a SmartArt graphic where the text that appears in the SmartArt graphic can be entered and edited.

**Wizard** A feature that asks questions and then creates an item according to the provided answers.

# Index

 The internet icon represents Index entries found within More Skills
on the companion website: www.prenhall.com/skills